The Happy, Fun, Party Travel Guide to Reno

A Guide to Casinos, Bars, Restaurants, and Special Events in Reno and Sparks

2018

by Ed SJC Park

2018 First Edition: January 2018

ISBN 978-1-304-18668-3

Acknowledgements

Stacey S, Dennis F, Robert H, Eric L, Tom C, Brad D, Kevin L, Tyra C, Kristen S, Rachel M, Jay B, Eric H, Scott B, Leslie B, Laura F, Ingrid M, and Nick V my drinking buddies and those who helped me get around to all the bars in Reno, Sparks, and Sun Valley. Robert H was the one who convinced me to move to Reno and Stacey S came up with the idea of hitting every bar in Reno.

If you enjoy this book, check out other books by Ed SJC Park:

Novels

The Bill Keane Series

      eGo: A Dot-com Bubble Story (set in Reno, Nevada)

      CDO: A Story about Selling Collateralized Debt Obligations

      GOD from the Machine (set in Las Vegas, Nevada)

      Zen: Life and Death in the Biggest Little City (set in Reno, Nevada)

Keno in Reno (set in Reno, Nevada)

The Path of Our Sacred Delusions

Soul Crushing (set in Reno, Nevada)

Table of Contents

Introduction

Some might argue that travel guides are history. I would agree, and that is why this is not your traditional travel guide. If you want to know the basics and history of a city, you can go to Wikipedia. When I used to buy travel guides, I probably only read a few dozen pages. My main interest was the restaurants and nightlife. Almost half my book is dedicated to restaurants and nightlife. Travel guides mostly ignore them, because first, most travel guide writers are boring old codgers. Second, the restaurants and bars are always changing along with the scene. I have been updating this book at least annually since it came out in 2012.

Why not just use Yelp, Tripadvisor, Google Maps or one of any online reviews? The majority of these reviewers are still chained to chain restaurants. You're taking advice from people who usually eat junk food, factory food, and corporate pink slime. I am not a fine dining snob. I am however conscious of what I eat, and I am drawn to natural, sustainable, local, independent, organic, trustworthy, hormone-free, grass-fed, bio-diverse, inventive, eclectic, and authentic cuisine. Having lived in Reno since 1995, I know the hidden gems, and I am always on the hunt for more. Additionally, I am a party fiend, and by 2012, I had been to every single bar in Reno, Sparks, and Sun Valley (excluding restaurant and casino bars). This is the new age of exciting and fun party, travel guides.

If you've been living in a cave the last few years, you probably haven't noticed the growing trend toward local, sustainable, independent culture, cuisine, and lifestyle. There are cool, hipster neighborhoods sprouting up all over from Brooklyn to Mission in San Francisco. Reno has one too called Midtown. This is our fastest growing bohemian, hipster, indie cultural center. If you live in Reno, you might want to read this guide just to familiarize yourself with the new Reno culture. You might think it's oh so tight pants, thick glasses, and fixie bike posing and trendsterism, but you don't have to dress like that to enjoy the resurgence of natural, trustworthy, sustainable, independent, and local cuisine and culture. In a day and age where big business and banks want us to subsidize them and then allow them to impoverish and poison us, I'd rather put on some tight pants and rebel alongside the kids, live free and healthy, and flourish.

Reno is also getting a lot of national media attention lately:

http://www.nytimes.com/2014/07/07/business/reno-nevada-recasts-itself-as-home-to-tech-start-ups.html?_r=0

http://www.nytimes.com/2013/10/20/travel/a-reno-neighborhood-drinks-in-style.html

http://www.sfgate.com/wine/spirits/article/Reno-rolls-the-dice-on-a-serious-cocktail-culture-5879321.php

http://www.sfgate.com/renotahoe/article/Reno-s-luck-and-local-scene-finally-5778387.php

http://www.huffingtonpost.com/findery/the-biggest-little-underr_b_5575088.html

http://www.theglobeandmail.com/life/travel/destinations/renos-incredible-revamp-if-you-havent-been-here-lately-maybe-you-should/article21992059/

http://www.usatoday.com/story/travel/destinations/2013/08/19/burning-man-festival-reno-public-art/2671427/

http://www.wsj.com/articles/reno-sees-future-and-it-isnt-casinos-1445642382

http://www.funnyordie.com/videos/c46bacd6e0/overly-excited-tourist-finds-renos-secret-wonders

All the photos in this book except on the cover were taken by me. If you want a good look at Reno in photos, go to:

www.downtownmakeover.com/downtown_reno_gallery_surreal.asp

Other resources to find out what's new in Reno are:

www.downtownmakeover.com

www.facebook.com/ThisIsReno

www.facebook.com/#!/groups/renofoodies/

Why Reno?

So why should I visit Reno? Why not Vegas? Sure, I've been to Vegas over a dozen times and enjoyed it, but sometimes the whole overblown, pretentious, expensive, sleazy, kitschy, gaudy, big fat corporate, dirty Disneyesque feel can get tiring. Vegas is like corporate America gone insane, while Reno is natural, local, authentic, and mostly independent. Some of our largest casinos here are still privately owned: Peppermill, Atlantis, and CalNeva. And seriously, I cannot tell you how many times I talk to a woman at a bar in Vegas only to find out she's a prostitute. The single women only hang out at nightclubs where it's $50 and one hour to get in, the drinks are overpriced, and they all cling together or hangout at VIP tables where you can't even talk to them. As far as I'm concerned, everyone expects way too much out of Vegas, and that's when the whole thing starts feeling like a party balloon slowing deflating. People in Reno are down-to-earth. It's not about what fashion label is wearing you, what sports car is driving you, or whatever status symbol owns you. You don't have to blow a couple weeks' wages to get attention, and even then, someone blowing a month's wages is getting more attention. And what kind of attention exactly are you after? For much, much less, you can have a great all-night party in Reno and gamble too. Reno is not only more genuine and less pretentious; it's more historic and authentic. Unlike Vegas, we're not blowing ourselves up and reinventing ourselves every few years.

When you first travel, you hit all the big cities, tick off all the big names: New York, LA, San Francisco, London, Paris, Tokyo, Seoul, Sydney, Vegas, Miami. At some point, you have bragging rights. Oh yeah, seen Big Ben, Eiffel Tower, Times Square, Hollywood, blah, blah, blah. After a while, it's not so much about the big names and bragging rights as it is about the actual experience, and that's when you start noticing the cracks in big cities: huge tourist traps, interacting mostly with tourists instead of locals, $300 a night hotels, overpriced snacks laid out all over the damn room which really annoys me when I'm blacked out drunk, overpriced drinks, overpriced low quality food, crowds, commute time, unfriendly people, long lines, panhandlers, scam-artists, crime, intense poverty, and when I encounter some famous landmark, snap a few photos, I stand there awkwardly amongst tourists going: is there a certain amount of time I'm supposed to be standing here taking this in before I can leave? A minute, 5, 10, 15? Seriously?

After a while, you start to see the beauty, cost benefits, and charm of smaller cities. In big cities, you go to a bar or restaurant, and chances are, staff are muttering, "damn tourist" and you get treated as such. They're tired of the culture clash, sign language, misunderstandings, returned food, meaningless transient nature of the interaction. In fact, in many Tokyo bars they will just outright ban foreigners from entering. When you go to a smaller city, you're a novelty not a nuisance. Staff and fellow patrons alike are more likely to find you interesting, fascinating, entertaining, and funny. I've had just as great parties in medium-sized cities as the big ones. It's not the size of the party that matters; it's the size of the party in the people. Even in large cities, there's a growing trend where locals avoid the big party districts, because they know it will be full of annoying tourists or local "party-commuters."

So go to Vegas, do your *Hangover* thing, whatever you do there, yeah, keep it there or get tested to make sure you didn't bring it back with you, but then come check out Reno, the Biggest Little City in the World. What does that mean? I mean, what is the biggest little car in the world? Aren't all midsize cars the biggest little cars? Okay, I'll explain the slogan. Back in the mid-20th century Reno was a small town, but because of legalized gambling, it attracted world class entertainers like Sinatra and Sammy Davis, Jr. Reno was Vegas before Vegas. America's wealthiest vacationed in Reno, and they brought a much higher level of sophistication and taste than a city the size of Reno could ever justify. Hence, our restaurants, bars, nightlife, and entertainment venues matched or exceeded those of big cities while our population made us a small city. With a huge influx of Bay Area culture and tourism, Reno still has a better dining and nightlife scene than any other city our size.

What is Reno?

Photo: downtown Reno looking north, Truckee River below

Reno is near the border of California and 4,500 feet high in the Sierra Nevada mountain range, 220 miles (driving) northeast of San Francisco, 450 miles northwest of Las Vegas, 36 miles northeast of Lake Tahoe, 23 miles west of the Tesla Gigafactory, and 17 miles west of the Mustang Ranch brothel. There are about 245 thousand folks here, another 98 thousand next door in Sparks and as the saying goes, "Reno is so close to hell you can see Sparks." Both cities are part of Washoe County which goes from Lake Tahoe all the way up to the Oregon border 250 miles away and has about 454 thousand people. Unlike counties out east, our counties are larger than some of your puny states! You could fit the entire state of Connecticut inside Washoe County. And our state has more land mass than the United Kingdom! Yeah, I don't know what constitutes the United Kingdom, Northern Ireland? But still, the United Kingdom! There are about 3 million people in the entire state of Nevada, more than Brooklyn! 85% of Nevada land is federally owned including a few hundred square miles of an irradiated nuclear bomb test range near Las Vegas (again 450 miles away from Reno). Even the Communist Cuban federal government doesn't own 85% of all their land. Nevada also has Area 51's Groom Lake military base, the most well-known secret base in the universe and home to a community of 73 aliens, mostly illegal. Reno is the 3rd largest city in Nevada after Henderson.

Reno 911 Trailer Trash Reputation

Well, thanks to the TV show "Reno 911" the improvisational version of *Police Academy* the movie, or more recently *Kingpin, Balls of Fury* or *The Muppet Movie*, Reno has an ill-deserved reputation as this trailer trash, home of third-rate, has-been Vegas acts, broken dreams, despair, a dirty cheap hillbilly cousin of Vegas, a back alley cauldron of meth and heroin junkies, a wannabe hipster grotto, and a 24-hour sin-hole with Carol Channing turning tricks on 4th Street for a dime bag.

So what's there to like about Reno? Reno has the great outdoors which far surpass the desert wastelands of Vegas. Fewer than half the people who live here were born here. We're half-bred not inbred. About half are California immigrants, myself included, and before the Great Recession, Reno was actually one of the fastest growing cities in America if not the world. For quite some time, Reno was the Venice of the Western states. Okay, maybe Pisa or something. No, Reno doesn't have a leaning building, but we did once have a ridiculous leaning Christmas tree in 2010.

We don't all live in trailer homes and drive a jacked up pickup with a pit bull on the front seat. I used to call Reno the Far East Bay, a distant exurb of the Bay Area along the I-80 corridor, but we're more of a hybrid with the dusty, rural, NRA-registered, freedom-loving Northern Nevadans. I like to think that we wed the sophistication and multiculturalism of Northern California with the down-to-earth, bucolic charm of Northern Nevada.

After the Great Recession, however, Reno suffered greatly. Reno official unemployment maxed out at 13.9% in 2011 while Nevada maxed out at 13.7% in 2010. On top of this, the unemployment rate only follows people who have sought employment in the last four weeks and exclude those who have simply given up. Reno has fully rebounded now with unemployment under 4%. Many innovative, new restaurants and bars have opened in the last several years among them restaurants: Liberty Food & Wine Exchange, Bab Café, Centro, Uchi Ramen, Kauboi Izakaya, Washoe Public House, Laughing Planet; nightclubs LEX and NoVi; bars: The Eddy, Blind Dog Tavern, The Stick, Faces, and Press Start; and Whitney Peak Hotel which includes Roundabout restaurant, concert venue Cargo, and an outdoor climbing wall that scales the entire 16-story building. Reno is experiencing a great transformation from big box, chain store, strip mall Cali-land to more independent, authentic, innovative, eclectic, and sustainable businesses.

And California businesses still see big tax breaks moving across the border. So long as Northern California remains the leader of global technology and Reno keeps its taxes low, Reno will always thrive. In addition to attracting a sizeable server farm for Apple, we are home to Tesla's Gigafactory a lithium battery factory at the Tahoe-Reno Industrial Center (TRI) nine miles east of Reno. While some may argue that our $1.25 billion in tax breaks for Tesla is government-big business collusion and unfair to smaller businesses, it's better than decades of virtually subsidizing dying downtown Reno gaming in the form of a bowling stadium, convention center, the train trench, and the Aces baseball stadium and entertainment complex.

Although, our casino and hotel industry have been declining, they have been in decline for some time even while Reno's economy was booming. Casino and hotel employment makes up less than 7% of total local employment compared to 16% in 1996. While our casino sector is shrinking, people overlook the growing restaurant and bar sector. According to the Nevada Department of Employment, Training, and Rehabilitation, casino and hotel employment has dropped from over 27K in 1995 to 14.2K in 2017. **Meanwhile, food and drinking service employment has nearly doubled from over 8K in 1995 to 16.9K in 2017.** Reno no longer really needs the casino and hotel industry to succeed. Reno is increasingly becoming a more innovative, sustainable, family-oriented place to live not just to visit. However, if you are visiting Reno, you should not only visit the casinos downtown but also the restaurants, bars, and shops Midtown, our fast-growing, most innovative, independently-owned, boutique-bohemian neighborhood. Some call it hipster, but we'll talk about that later.

Where did Reno come from?

Photo: This is not an old photo of Reno. I'm too cheap to pay for some old photo. I took this recently and applied the old photo style on it using an app.

Let's get a little historical here, we're talking Wild West when some dude named Mark Twain was riding his horse around and maybe hit a few saloons, brothels and opium dens. Back then, there was a Silver Rush in 1859 following the California Gold Rush of 1849. Imagine all the single dudes inundating the area seeking their quick fortune and all the scam-artists. What do single dudes want back in 1859? There's no Nintendo, World of Warcraft, Fantasy Football, Facebook, skateboards or pot. Well, you guessed it: booze, whores, opium, and gambling.

Back then the big towns were Carson City and Virginia City. Reno was more like a pit stop to cross the Truckee River where some dude named Myron Lake made a killing charging tolls for his bridge. In 1870, Reno had 1,035 people while Carson City had 3,042 and Virginia City had 7,048 (not including Gold Hill down the road with 4,311 people). Las Vegas didn't even make the census until 1920 with 2,304 people. At some point, it was trendy to name your city after some Civil War Union general, so Reno chose obscure Union General Jesse L. Reno. His ancestors changed his named from Renault to Reno, so had they not we might be called Renault today. The town of Reno became official on May 13, 1868 after Myron Lake deeded land to Central Pacific Railroad realizing that after the Transcontinental Railroad was finished he could further his fortunes by making Reno a railroad depot. Central Pacific maintained facilities further east, and the town built around that became Sparks.

In 1931, Reno was truly born when the Great Depression inspired Nevadans to promote the place as the gambling and divorce capital of America. Nevada legalized gambling and to get a divorce, all you had to do was live in Nevada for six weeks. Hordes of gamblers and divorce-seeking women descended upon the city turning it into a big party town. Marilyn Monroe would later make a movie about a divorcee in Reno called the *Misfits* in 1961. The Rat Pack was often doing gigs here as well as Vegas. By the end of the 1950's however, the Vegas population had surpassed Reno's and never looked back. In 1979, Reno further sealed their fate as a runner up to Vegas when citizens voted in "managed-growth" politicians including mayoral candidate and community activist Barbara Bennett, and major casino projects shifted focus to Vegas. Now, you can say this is where Reno screwed up, but seriously, for locals, do you think they really wanted to turn their backyard into the Disneyesque sin city that Vegas has become?

Instead, California businesses simply discovered Reno as a great tax haven kind of like Europeans view Switzerland, and our ski resorts are just as nice. During the previous Recession in the 1990's, unlike most of the nation and especially California, Reno continued to grow, getting another population influx from unemployed Californians, myself included. Reno grew 33% from 1990 to 2000, however, gaming and tourism starting slowing down by the late 90's. The dot com and housing boom then propped up Reno further so it could be pushed off a cliff in 2008 with the Great Recession. This was the first time Reno's population and economy actually shrunk. Along with Vegas and Miami, we got drunk off our asses on the dizzying acceleration of real estate prices planning high-rise condos all along the Truckee River. Credit was so loose and wild, I kid you not, I had a friend with no job, no assets, no car, loads of debt, previously couldn't even qualify for a cellphone and all the sudden he's getting offers for a $200K home loan. No kidding!

When the Great Recession hit, Reno and Vegas unemployment were the highest in the nation. We were closer to the brink of a Great Depression than any place in America. I remember reading Middle School textbooks about the Great Depression and looking at photos of long soup lines, and never did I imagine I'd wind up volunteering to work a long soup line in Reno. No new casino has opened since Silver Legacy in 1995, and many others have closed since 1995 including Eddie's Fabulous 50's, the Virginian, Nevada Club, Riverboat, Comstock, Flamingo Hilton (which became the Golden Phoenix which failed), Sundowner, Speakeasy, Rocky's, Fitzgeralds, little ol' Old Reno Casino, and Siena most recently. The only remaining casinos in downtown Reno are Silver Legacy, Eldorado, Circus Circus, Harrah's, CalNeva, Little Nugget, and Sands.

Siri's Casino also opened replacing what was once the Virginia Street entrance to the Golden Phoenix and the Flamingo Hilton before that.

However, as mentioned above, hotel and gaming have become an increasingly small part of our economy and the future of Reno lies in attracting new business to Reno and providing them with a wide range of innovative, eclectic, independently-owned, sustainable restaurants, bars, and retail stores to keep them here.

Note: To find out what caused the Great Recession read former Goldman Sachs executive director, Greg Smith's resignation letter published in the New York Times:

http://www.nytimes.com/2012/03/14/opinion/why-i-am-leaving-goldman-sachs.html?_r=1&hp.

Read the brilliant books by Charles R. Morris, *The Two Trillion Dollar Meltdown,* Dylan Ratigan's *Greedy Bastards,* or David Stockman's *The Great Deformation.* Why the digression? Wall Street really screwed over Reno, and this is my payback. I'm not asking for an Occupy Wall Street 12-point reform of the Capitalist system; I'm asking for a 2-point reform: greater regulation of the derivatives market and reenacting the Glass-Steagall Act separating commercial and investment banking. No more mind-boggling, Alice in Wonderland derivatives dreamed up by coked-up Wall Street bankers and sociopathic quantum physicists turned quantitative analysts. Greed is still good, as Gordon Gecko says, but it is exploitation, manipulation, deception, and law-breaking that is bad and that is what caused the Great Recession.

One of the best modern history books about Reno I ever read is called **The Roots of Reno** by Al Moe. It's only $2.99 as an eBook. Do yourself a favor, it's an astonishing look at a very shady time. "King" George Wingfield is truly the father of not only modern gaming Reno but Lake Tahoe as well. He moved to Reno in 1908 and later brought in Nick Abelman, Bill Graham, and Jim McKay to help him run casinos and banks. They all had connections with Chicago mobsters. Abelman was probably the least worst, keeping clear of killings and con jobs but none-the-less aided and abetted his buddies. It also covers Sinatra allegedly drugging Marilyn Monroe at his Cal Neva Lodge at Lake Tahoe. A few days later, she was found dead in Los Angeles perhaps a result of what happened at Lake Tahoe. What you discover in this book is that Reno was built upon some pretty sick and evil things, but then again, our Founding Fathers owned slaves. Times have really changed, or have they?

Reno Demographic Culture

So what are Renoites like? What is Reno culture? Most people think Renoites are trailer trash or casino junkies, a few tourists thrown in. Let's start with the facts. As mentioned before, about half are from California. Less than a quarter were born here. About 17% are foreign born (Mexico and an assortment of Latin American countries). The rest are from many Western states and then a smattering from east of the Mississippi and a small percentage from the rest of the world. Latinos make up about 20% of the population. Asians make up about 6% and the most conspicuously small population are blacks at only 3%. How is that possible when just next door they make up 6% and Asians make up 13% of the California population?

One simple explanation is that Reno was not called the "Mississippi of the West" because they had good Southern comfort food and Waffle House. We don't have Waffle House, although gloriously we had Krispy Kreme donuts from 2001 to 2008. Reno had been a notoriously racist place for quite some time. Unlike Eastern cities, there was really nothing for non-whites to do around here. Gold and silver mining were often restricted only to whites. While the Chinese helped build the great Transcontinental Railroad, after work was done in 1869, many found themselves settling Western lands where they were viewed as foreign and hostile as the beloved Native Americans, except the Native Americans could retreat to their reservations. The Chinese eked out a living with Chinese restaurants, laundries, prostitution, a casino here or there, and opium dens, but for the most part were despised and purged out. In Reno, the city burned down Chinatown twice, twice! in 1878 and 1908. Vigilantes took it down in 1878 but city officials destroyed it in 1908 claiming it was for sanitary purposes, but seriously, imagine burning down the Tenderloin in San Francisco or the entire city of Detroit for sanitary purposes? To this day, I believe the area around the Truckee River and Lake Street, the old Reno Chinatown is cursed. Besides countless murders and fatal accidents in this area, the Mizpah hotel was burned down in 2006 killing twelve on Halloween. In 2011, three people were shot and killed in the area including a university football athlete. ALL in the same four square block area. I'm like the worst Reno salesperson so far right? Wait for it.

Blacks fared no better and most casinos were whites-only. They were restricted to a small neighborhood just northeast of downtown around Pat Baker Park and limited to low-level casino jobs: porters, dishwashers, or celebrity acts like Sammy Davis, Jr. who could perform at a casino only to be thrown out and spend the night at a mixed-race casino hotel.

Needless to say, blacks and Asians have passed over Reno for the more minority-friendly state of California. However, we're talking a few generations back, and today, black and Asian tourists flock to Reno without the slightest clue as to our sordid racist past. In fact, with the high number of black and Asian tourists already cruising around downtown, they inadvertently assume that there are a lot of blacks and Asians living in Reno, at least that's what I thought before moving here.

The Latinos who helped build the cities of Vegas and Reno, doing all the jobs behind the scenes, make up the largest minority population, and despite occasional outbursts of gang activity, the vast majority of Latinos are law-abiding, hardworking good people. Some people worry about Latino culture taking over America, but just like the 2nd, 3rd, 4th generation Irish, Chinese, Italians (think Jersey Shore), Iranians (think Shahs of Sunset), Armenians (think Kardashian) they all become as American as anyone else and get their own reality TV show.

The real minorities in Reno are actually the rural whites who were born in Northern Nevada, in small towns besides Reno and Sparks, including Stead, Sun Valley, Lemmon Valley, Carson City, Fernley, Minden, Gardnerville, Yerington, Fallon, and Winnemucca. Some may derogatorily refer to them as white trash or trailer trash. (Do yourself another favor and read *White Trash: The 400-Year Untold History of Class in America* by Nancy Isenberg. Dividing and conquering the poor has been going on a lot longer than you think.) Back in the day, this area was filled with ranchers and cowboys and the heritage continues in rural communities and the North Valleys of Reno. Their children still embrace the country lifestyle: country homes, country music, line dancing, Western clothes, Sarah Palin, Larry the Cable Guy, etc. Oddly enough, if there's one group of people that urban whites discriminate against and excoriate the most it is their brethren rural whites. Ironically, many urban whites start off as rural whites.

Funny enough, the largest immigrant population is not Latin American but Californian, mostly Northern Californians. Northern Californians are similar to people in most large urban areas in America but both geographically and culturally a hybrid of their southern Californian counterparts and Portlandigans and Seattleites up north. Because of the Silicon Valley influence, many are highly educated and technologically savvy. In general, they tend to be more left-wing and progressive than Northern Nevadans. It is interesting to note that Reno has become one of the most hotly contested election cities in America. Vegas is mostly Democrat while the rest of Nevada is Republican, however, it is Reno the hybrid leftist-conservative town that often decides which way the entire state will go. For a town of 350K, Presidential candidates spend disproportionate time rubbing elbows in some of our quaint, old-fashioned restaurants catering to the old folk who vote. No, they will never visit a hipster grotto.

Notable Micro-Ethnic Communities

I'm sure most medium-sized cities have bizarre, random micro-ethnicities, and Reno is no exception. Our traditional large ethnic groups are Italians, Basque, and Greek. The obvious large ethnic groups are Mexicans and El Salvadorans. Because the casinos used to employ a lot of Polish workers in the summer and Brazilian workers in the winter, we have a lot of stragglers left over from that. I'm not sure why, but we have a lot of Filipinos who work in the casino industry and in the medical field. I also don't know why we have a large Pacific Island community: Hawaiians, Samoans, Fijians, and Micronesians. One clue is that a lot of our university football players are Pacific Islanders and many stay in Reno after a career of uncompensated concussions. For whatever reason, many also become sushi chefs. There is a Korean community in Sparks. You can't really call New Yorkers an ethnic group, but we also have a lot of people from New York who have opened bars, delis, Italian restaurants, and pizza places. Back in the 30's, many New Yorkers moved here. Reno truly was one of the most sophisticated, cultured cities out west back then. Many books written in the 30's mention Reno. Also, back then they called nightclubs "café's" and often wore tuxedos to them.

There used to be a lot of Japanese exchange students at the University of Nevada, and it used to be so funny how they were by far the most stylish youth in Reno. Most college students wear the basic dress code of t-shirts, jeans, baggy shorts for dudes or virtual underwear shorts for women. Some Japanese students were all Harajuku'd out, but of course, not as crazy as goth Lolita. There are also Native Americans including one colony that sits right in the middle of Reno near the Grand Sierra that includes Paiute, Shoshone, and Washoe tribes. They have an Indian Smoke Shop. In October 2010 they opened a Wal-Mart store on their property in exchange for a bag of Walmart grapes. A portion of the tax revenue will go to the Nevada Department of Corrections and Washoe County School District, so if you must shop at Walmart, shop there!

Is Reno a Hipster Wannabe Town?

Reno is the least most ironic and well-known obscure, unhipster hipster town in the world.

It seems these days, calling someone a hipster is a big insult, and it is, but it's complicated. Let's be clear here, someone who recycles, cares about the environment, drives a hybrid, buys local and at independent stores, eats at independent restaurants, and doesn't jump on the corporate commercialist bandwagon buying up the latest pop culture crap is a pretty cool person. That is the essence and ideal of true hipsterism, but the problem is that a lot of so-called hipsters only pose and dress as hipsters and are full of stupid contradictions. So you have a dude who wears tight red pants, thick black glasses, has a tat sleeve, a moustache, but he drinks PBR which is owned by a corporate beer conglomerate. He drives a brand new car with a V8. He doesn't recycle. He buys all his hipster clothes new. He eats fast food all the time. He's not a real hipster. He's just a poseur, a fake, a trendster, someone who only dresses like a hipster to get the benefits of being a hipster without paying the true costs. It was just like with hippies. There were hippies that only dressed like hippies, and there were hippies who were out there protesting the war, fighting for civil rights, doing psychedelics for spiritual reasons, and living in communes.

That is why real hipsters don't like being called hipsters and why it has become an insult. Reno is both good at being true hipster lifestyle and fake hipster fashion. Renoites are discovering local food, independent stores and restaurants, recycling, conservation, sustainability, smart growth, living close to work, riding bicycles more, etc. But there are plenty of Renoites who just imitate the fashion and lifestyle trends from Portland and San Francisco, not because they care about their health or the planet, but because they want to desperately fit in and look cool.

But as far as I'm concerned, I'd rather have youth pretending to be environmental conservationists promoting the local, independent economy than the last big trend: youth pretending to be gangster thugs, rapists, murderers, drug dealers, pimps, and general assholes. I mean seriously, wouldn't you rather walk down an alley and run into a dozen hipster wannabes making sarcastic, snide remarks about your yuppie fashion sensibilities or would you rather run into a dozen gangbanger wannabes jacking you up for your wallet?

What is the Food Like in Reno?

Well, that all depends, what do you want? There was a time, pre-2005, when there wasn't much of a food scene in Reno, just like the old paltry beer scene. It was chain and corporate this and that. Reno has been transformed. It's still not Portland, Seattle, or San Francisco, but it is definitely better than any city the same size I've ever been.

Now first of all, let's talk food. Just like beer, most Americans eat the same corporate shit and drink the same corporate shit and then shit and piss out corporate waste while their livers retain the remainder of the toxic corporate slime. One of my favorite pastimes was salivating and awaiting the opening of chains in Reno: California Cheesecake Factory, Five Guys, Steak'n Shake, In'n'Out, Fat Burgers (not here anymore), Fuddrucker's, Krispy Kreme (not here anymore), PF Chang, Popeye's, Mel's Diner. I'm still waiting for Waffle House, White Castle, Umami Burger, and Hooter's (we had one once). Why do Americans love the same old stuff at the same old chains? The answer may surprise you. Before cars and interstate freeways, Americans didn't travel much and were actually poor. Today we think we're entitled to great food and beer, but back then, food was sustenance not luxury. They ate what their mothers cooked.

As Americans began to drive cross country, their greatest fear was encountering some unknown hotel or restaurant and getting poor quality or ripped off. As a result, regional, then national chains offered Americans reliability and safety. Denny's in New York would provide you with the same menu, same price, and same customer service as Denny's in Atlanta or Los Angeles, so if you were new in Atlanta, you went to Denny's. America became the land of chains. And who can really blame them? It's 1960, you're poor, you got $3 to spend on dinner, the heck you're going to waste it on spoiled meat in a mom-and-pop grease spoon by the highway.

The Internet is changing all that. Let's say you're on business travel to Atlanta now, and hey, there's a Denny's. You know exactly what you're getting. But you've heard about great Southern cooking and want to try it out, but you don't want to walk into some local joint where you may get ripped off or poor food quality. Yelp! That's right, Yelp! You find a nice looking local restaurant and you Yelp! There are mostly good reviews, they love some item on the menu you've never even heard of, so what do you do? Google it! Standardization is now bad, uniqueness and regionalism and independently-owned, good.

Restaurant and bar owners can now experiment with whole new items, because customers, especially now with their smart phones, can look it up. What the heck is an espetada? Google it! What the hell is a solyanka? Google it! What the heck is a Baltika 7? Google it! Now, more than ever, people are finally embracing the esoteric and authentic. We're talking about food people ate a long time ago in their native lands. I guarantee you, within the next twenty years, Americans will not only start eating more and more exotic foods, but more and more exotic meats: lamb, buffalo, all sorts of fish (not just tuna, salmon or cod), liver, wild boar, sea urchins, sea slugs, turtles, insects, you name it. Andrew Zimmern won't be the only American eating crazy shit, although just watching that dude scarf down a hotdog makes me queasy. Can they please turn off his mic when he's eating?

Besides getting greater variety and more authentic global cuisine, what else is the big deal with this new hipster food trend? You should pick yourself up an incredibly important food book called, *Omnivore's Dilemma*. It explains why we are pumping cows full of hormones and antibiotics, why factory food is simply not good for us. Not only are Americans becoming historically overweight and obese, we are also become historically sicker from the food we eat. Factory farming is also unsustainable and actually harms the environment. It is not only more responsible to eat local, natural, and sustainable food, but it is also better for our health. Some people argue that fast food and chain food is cheaper, but in the long run if you consider health costs and quality of life, investing in fast food and chain food is like creating a long-term investment portfolio that only involves gambling at a blackjack table. If you believe in free-market Capitalism, that we should allow people to choose freely to eat garbage, then we should also not be subsidizing factory farms and foods, and we should not subsidize the healthcare for people who make themselves sick with unhealthy diets. Another awesome book is *Brain Maker: The Power of Gut Microbes to Heal and Protect Your Brain-for Life* by David Perlmutter. You have no idea how bad antibiotics are until you read this book. Also watch the documentary *Cowspiracy* which uncovers the water-intensive, land-destroying, unsustainable practice of raising livestock.

There used to be a time when we could trust chains to provide consistent quality and service, however, those days are long gone. As global, corporate conglomerates eat up chain restaurants, they are more concerned with cutting labor and food costs resulting in worse service and questionable food quality, replacing as many natural ingredients with artificial ingredients and then to compensate for less taste, loading food with unhealthy salt, trans fats, and corn syrup. In 2013, both the Carrow's and Denny's on Plumb Lane received a food inspection score of 78 out of 100 (the second lowest restaurant scores in two years).

We also owe a lot of the modern organic, natural, fresh, local food movement to Alice Waters who opened Chez Panisse in 1971 and ever since, it has been one of the most highly praised and awarded restaurants in the world. Alice Waters is one of the most important pioneers of California Cuisine and creator of gourmet "designer" thin crust pizza which Wolfgang Puck and California Pizza Kitchen helped popularize. California Cuisine can be viewed as European culinary techniques and style applied to any popular cuisine found in California. As California Cuisine has spread to all parts of America along with the California health food craze, many now refer to this type of cuisine as New American. It is basically gourmet culinary techniques applied to popular foods you can find all over America including Chinese, Thai, Japanese, Mexican, Southern, Cajun, Indian, and Mediterranean as well as all types of popular American foods like burgers, hot dogs, pizzas, crab cakes, casseroles, meatloaf, sandwiches, subs, BBQ, and cupcakes.

What are the Best Restaurants in Reno?

Reno is slowly getting there, and I will share with you the few notable restaurants that are offering quality, exotic, innovative, fresh, and authentic food. People should also keep in mind that while today's youth like to spend their money on electronics, partying, and fashion, more and more are discovering the wild and wonderful world of traveling and gourmet dining. Not only are chefs becoming more inventive and creative, but their customers' tastes are becoming more eclectic and open. Of highest importance is natural, whole, organic, and farm fresh foods.

THE TEN BEST

(in no particular order)

Campo

50 N Sierra St, 4 Star

Some say "Campo" like it rhymes with "sample" and some say "Campo" like it rhymes with "mambo." Some say "Pho" like it rhymes with "Joe" and some say "Pho" like it rhymes with "duh." Who cares? There are scientific studies that you can only learn certain sounds as an infant, so it's culturally insensitive to impose any native pronunciation on others. Anyway, Campo makes their own cured meats and has fresh ingredients from local farms. The interior is a bit too hipster for me but they have a very innovative, authentic small Italian menu. No endless breadsticks and fettuccini Alfredo here.

There are two people in Reno who share a great deal of responsibility for Reno's great new culture. **Jessica Schneider**, owner of Junkee Clothing and creator of an old local television show, *Reno Style*, is arguably the founder of Midtown Reno, anchoring her store there and aggressively promoting the area. **Mark Estee**, former owner of Reno Local Food Group, a local conglomerate of restaurants and food retailers including Campo, Heritage (now Roundabout), Chez Louie at Nevada Museum of Art, Burger Me, and Reno Provisions (now Liberty Food & Wine Exchange). All his restaurants served local, natural, sustainable, healthy food. Unfortunately, he overextended himself with Reno Provisions and had to sell Campo and Heritage, but his contributions cannot be overlooked especially during the worst economic period in Reno history. He recently opened Liberty Food & Wine Exchange. With 60% of restaurants failing within the first three years, think of restaurateurs more as local charity workers than profiteers.

Lulou's

1470 South Virginia St, 4 Star

For those who don't mind spending a little more for what added value comes from being at one of the most expensive restaurants in Reno (outside the casino steakhouses), it has some of the best, eclectic, and healthy foods in Reno. The décor is more *Sex and the City* than hipsterdom which I actually like especially for a romantic dinner unless of course you're dating a hipster who will only appreciate the décor ironically. Their relatively large Willamette Valley Pinot Noir wine bottle listing is notable although I think they get a little too creative with their crab cakes and mac'n'cheese extracting the necessary elements that make them classic favorites. An added bonus is their claim to have taken some of the staff from the old Sezmu, what used to be hands down the best restaurant in Reno. Both Sezmu and Theory were way ahead of their time in Reno and suffered from the Great Recession.

The Stone House Café

1907 S Arlington Ave, 4 Star

Stone House is a rock solid bistro. I don't know why restaurants call themselves 'café' which gives you the impression it's a coffee shop. Back in the 20's they called nightclubs 'cafés' which is even more confusing, but then again, if you went back to the 20's you wouldn't even understand anyone. "Darling, that café was the bee's knees, why I had a gay old time my dear boy all things considered, but I got so blotto off highballs I do say, don't be terribly cross poochy boo, why everyone got jingled. Bye the bye it was better than hoofing it round town with a bunch of teetotalers." Actually, I'm not even sure you can call this a bistro or grill or grille or whatever. It's an upscale seafood and steak place with lamb, chicken livers, escargot, and crab quesadilla's! The place was converted from a house. They serve breakfast from 7 AM to 4 PM! I would argue they have the best breakfast in town, but honestly I have not been to all the breakfast places in town, because I rarely get up early enough. Before Mark Estee, Reno had **Charlie Abowd** who opened this restaurant and Adele's in Carson City (the best restaurant in Carson City) and the old Adele's in Reno. (Another of Reno's greatest chefs is **Larry Dunning** who ran Sezmu, Rawr, Bowl, and Gamen Ramen.)

4th Street Bistro

3065 W 4th St, 4 Star

These guys were really the first true hipster, green, sustainable, regional restaurant in Reno opened in 2000. A great menu but a shitty location. The décor is dated, mostly because of the ugly, old French posters that were popular in college dorms in the 80's. Make a reservation, because this place is busy. Chef **Natalie Sellers** is another legendary Reno chef.

Beaujolais Bistro

753 Riverside Dr, 4 Star

Much like Midtown Eats, Beaujolais solved their biggest problem, space, by moving and expanding (formerly 130 West St). This is a classical French restaurant where the prices would be significantly higher in a larger city.

CHI

Peppermill, 4 Star

Usually, you shouldn't be impressed by a casino restaurant except for their steak and seafood restaurants which they smartly take care of for their big whales (gamblers who spend hundreds of thousands of dollars, a day!). Them big whales loves them their filet mignon and lobster and Rombauer Chards. As far as the buffets for the working class and diners for their late night drunks, the food is subpar. CHI is amazing and authentic Chinese. Yes, they too have General's Chicken, of course. I don't know exactly who General Tso was, but I'm pretty sure he never went to military school and put his life on the line in epic battles to wind up the Colonel Sanders of American-Chinese dining. CHI has expensive and exotic fare like sea cucumber, abalone, and fish maw (fish air bladder). Locals can get dining coupons by signing up for a player's card to buffer the wallet wallop. While Reno doesn't have a lot of local deals (Hash House a Go Go is the only one I know of), if you have a Nevada ID, a lot of Vegas casinos and clubs have big discounts for locals. Yes, living 450 miles from Vegas, you still count as a local.

Brasserie St. James

901 S. Center St, 4 Star

Brasserie is a huge place that uses its own water supply (formerly Crystal Springs water). At first this place struggled in both the microbrew and food department, but recently, and commendably, their beers have made staggering improvements and have earned national acclaim. The food has always been hit-or-miss, but seems to be more hit than miss lately too even though the menu hasn't changed much since they opened. What puts the place over-the-top as one of the top ten in Reno is the simple fact that the place has a great vibe and plenty of bar space for solo diners with two rooms, one without televisions for a somewhat more laid back scene. They also have a huge upstairs, outdoor patio open in the summer.

Midtown Eats

18 Cheney St, 4 Star

Formerly at 719 S Virginia St, this place has fixed its only flaw, a cramped dining area. Their lamb burgers are a favorite, but their cocktails are on another level. To showcase their cocktails, they created the cocktail bar **Death & Taxes**. If you know any cocktail aficionado, you need to take them to **Death & Taxes** and **Chapel Tavern**.

Louis' Basque Corner

301 E 4th St, 4 Star

For its size, Reno has a large Basque population. There are two Basque restaurants. Never really got Basque cuisine, just seems like American food: baked chicken and potatoes. This place, however, has cool esoteric dishes like rabbit and beef tongue. I asked someone once if your tongue goes numb, how do you know whether you're chewing beef tongue or your own tongue? Also, isn't it odd how we say beef instead of cow, veal instead of young cow, pork instead of pig, and mutton instead of lamb. One theory is that the Normans who invaded England in 1066 became the ruling class and could afford to eat cows, pigs, and sheep and hence referred to them in their French language, beouf, porc, mouton, whereas the conquered Anglos only raised the cows, pigs, and sheep and hence kept these words for the animals. To further complicate things, some Mexican taco trucks only use the word meat instead of beef as in meat taco.

The Depot Craft Brewery Distillery

325 E 4th St, 4 Star

Newly opened in an old railroad depot with parking in back off Evans Ave, this is a restaurant, microbrewery, and a craft distillery. New American menu with local ingredients. I remember when Satellite Bar opened in Reno which is now Loving Cup. It was the first modern, trendy, upscale bar Reno had in decades. It was a game changer. Then came 210 North, the first modern, trendy, upscale nightclub Reno had in decades. Another game changer. I would designate The Depot as yet another trendy benchmark in modern Reno history. When you're inside, you simply forget that you're in Reno. The immediate neighborhood is a wild and crazy coterie of a Burner hotel, homeless shelter, and Basque restaurant. However, don't get all snobby against the homeless just because you can afford to eat and drink at The Depot. Most of the annoying panhandlers downtown are not homeless, and most homeless people do not panhandle and are veterans with mental and psychological problems. When government fails to take care of the most vulnerable people in society, you don't blame these people, you don't blame government, you should do something. In a day and age of gourmet dining, never forget the privilege and responsibility of feeding those who cannot even afford a basic meal. I've mentioned a few famous Reno chefs who have fed the rich and well off, but I'd also like to mention **Amber Lynn Dodson** who feeds the homeless and those in need across the street from the Depot with her group **We Care Volunteers**.

You may have noticed my bias here. I like places that serve healthy raised, healthy food. I simply think it's irresponsible to eat animals that have been cruelly treated and fed foods that make them sick which then require loads of antibiotics which in turn is creating super bacteria which will one day kill us all if we don't first kill ourselves with poisoned food. You really are what you eat down to the atom and quark. When animals are stressed, not only do you ingest the bad karma, but you also ingest toxins the animals were too stressed to flush out of their system and you don't get as much nutrient which the animal is too stressed to absorb. Stressed animals also use up glycogen in their muscles. Glycogen makes the meat taste better and also increases lactic acid which creates an ideal pH in the meat and slows spoilage. Whether you believe in bad energy flow or science, they both agree, eating sick and stressed animals will make you sick and stressed.

All these restaurants except CHI and Louis' Basque serve New American food. This doesn't mean I'm culturally closed-minded. New American is like America itself and combines cuisines of the world. However, most ethnic restaurants simply haven't begun using healthier meats and outside of Italian, Spanish, and French ones, they tend to be cheaper places with cheaper décor and amenities. Also, since Reno is not exactly a worldly city, I don't rate many of the foreign restaurants highly here whereas I would give a much higher rating to the great Indian, Indonesian, or Peruvian restaurants of bigger cities like San Francisco.

THE REST OF THE BEST

(in no particular order)

Kauboi Izakaya

1286 S Virginia St

While sushi is king in Reno and trendy throughout the world, often overlooked is the Japanese Izakaya dining culture, comparable to the good, old-fashioned American diner. Check out the Netflix series, *Midnight Diner: Tokyo Stories* for a quick introduction to the Izakaya culture, sort of like *Cheers* if *Cheers* just served food. My theory is that they opened this place to serve the Japanese Panasonic workers who are in Reno and work at the new Tesla Gigafactory. You may not be aware that Panasonic is supplying the batteries for Tesla's cars and Powerwall. I love fish-out-of-water stories like *Crocodile Dundee* and wonder what the Japanese workers think of Reno and Renoites. Kauboi has eclectic, charcoal grilled items. Honestly don't be shy going into an "ethnic" restaurant. You may find that a lot of staff in "ethnic" restaurants seem to be a bit distant and formal, but American service staff is actually unique in the world in that they are more informal and friendly. In most of the rest of the world, service staff behaving informal and too friendly would be a sign of disrespect and imposition. Some trendy new places are trying to mimic the rest of the world by telling their staff to be less friendly and more formal, but my response to that is, well, like the rest of the world, I shouldn't tip here then?

Old Granite Street Eatery

243 S Sierra St, 4 Star

There's this new hipster interior design thing where the walls are bare except for perhaps an ugly drawing of an ugly girl with pigtails or a fat pig, exposed wood, exposed brick, restroom tiles for walls (Reno Public House), minimalist, hard wooden benches for seats, no table cloth. Despite this, the food here is local, fresh, and innovative. Hey hipster, I get it, fancy, warm interior design is associated with corporate restaurants and old-fashioned, upscale places. But seriously, a fricking wooden bench where the cushions are on the backrest not on the seats?

Bistro 7

7111 S Virginia St #B, 4 Star

Bistro 7's décor is the opposite of Campo. It is warm, elegant, sophisticated, sensual, flowing, rhythmic, and seductive. Okay, maybe old-fashioned 00's *Sex and The City* décor, but romantic is romantic, and Samantha is Samantha. The food is eclectic and they have a nice wine list.

Campo is about as romantic as a farm. Anyway, can we get some compromise hipsters? It's like with hipsters, the animals don't suffer but you do in cramped, ugly, noisy, exposed wooden and metal cages.

Ijji 2 Sushi and Japanese Steakhouse

4955 S. Virginia St, 4 Star

Reno is the all-you-can-eat sushi capital of the universe. In order to compete with the casino all-you-can-eat buffets, a sushi owner offered all-you-can-eat sushi and made a killing spawning dozens of copy cats. Predictably, Reno sushi is not all that great nor authentic. You won't find Toro in Reno, and I don't believe there's a single Japanese sushi chef in town. Most are Mexican or Polynesian. Most Reno sushi is deep-fried, crunchy rolls often filled with jalapenos and cream cheese. To get an idea of authentic sushi and the reverence placed upon it by Japanese culture, watch the documentary *Jiro Dreams of Sushi*. Some say that rice is the most important ingredient in sushi, but I think that's a bit of an exaggeration much like saying ice is the most important ingredient in a cocktail. It is the most overlooked and underappreciated ingredient, but trust me, if you have a nigiri with the best rice and mediocre tuna, it's worse than the best tuna and mediocre rice. Simply because of volume, many sushi places in Reno provide fresh seafood, but the vast majority provides old seafood that stinks and is often masked by the deep fryer. Basically, never order mackerel in Reno.

What puts Ijji 2 on the list is not their sushi but the teppanyaki dinner show. While their sushi is in the top three in the area, it's still all-you-can-eat which automatically downgrades the quality. Ichiban also has a teppanyaki dinner show, but there is no comparison. The show relies on a witty, crazy, audacious, wacky chef not only capable of astonishing feats with a knife but the ability to create a little party at the table with often unsuspecting guests getting food thrown at them and sake squirted into their mouths. Ichiban fails in this area while Ijji 2 triumphs fantastically.

Charlie Palmer's Steak

Grand Sierra Resort, 4 Star

Charlie Palmer is not only a chain with 18 locations, but it is also in a casino. Both these facts raise big red flags, but let us keep in mind why we hold our prejudices. Casino steakhouses are odious, old-school, uninspired 1960's (think *Fear and Loathing in Las Vegas*), Rombauer-swilling cesspits of old, rich whales or wealthy, middle-aged conventioneers who lack any taste or price-value appreciation. While there are hints of this here, I would have to say that Charlie Palmer exhibits the least number of symptoms and truly has exquisite meals.

Only the classic steaks are in the mid-30's while there are many mid-20 non-steak and seafood items including in the past Wagyu Beef Short Ribs. Wagwho? Wagyu covers several breeds of Japanese cows known for well-marbled delicious beef, the most notorious variety comes from the city of Kobe naturally known as Kobe beef. Wagyu does not necessarily come from Japan just as Angus does not necessarily come from Scotland. For solo/loner diners, there is a large lounge and bar area out front where you can catch a game on TV and not feel like a total loner schmuck. I think more restaurants should take advantage of the growing solo/loner diner market and set up a separate lounge and bar area.

The Grill at Quail Corners

6520 S McCarran Bl, 4 Star

After writing the first edition of this book in 2012, a friend scolded me for forgetting about this place. They have great ambiance, solid food, and sometimes live music. Southwest Reno used to be Reno's nicest neighborhood before even wealthier folks moved further south, but there is still a certain Southwest, white collar culture that is captured by this place.

Great Full Gardens Café and Eatery

555 S Virginia St, 4 Star

Although, I hate breakfast and lunch places, mostly because I rarely eat breakfast and lunch, this place is noteworthy for their fresh, local, and organic ingredients as well as a creative menu including liege waffles which are richer and sweeter than Belgian waffles. They do dinner, but it is limited to pastas.

The Twisted Fork

1191 Steamboat Pkwy, 4 Star

This restaurant offers an amazing eclectic menu including Kurobuta pork shoulder (the "Kobe beef" of pork), short ribs, cowboy rib eye, and prime hanger steak. The owners also own **Woody's Grill** which has surprising good food for a bar & grill. Unfortunately, they do not use grass-fed, hormone-free, holistic music-listening cows which may have put them in the top ten. They used to have a bartender lady who exhibits what I call "talent," a bartender who not only knows her drinks but has incredible customer service skills.

Hash House a Go Go

Harrah's, 4 Star

Again, weird name. You might think that this is some cheesy, chain casino restaurant that serves mediocre, greasy food, but you're only half right. They serve great food. I don't know why I keep thinking this is a breakfast place, probably because you associate hash with hash browns which you associate with breakfast, but this place serves impressive lunch and dinner, although their breakfast displays are probably the most famous part about them. The place has an indescribably fun vibe including serving a 24-oz beer in a paper bag. It's just a fun place to be where the starchy carb portions for breakfast will make you want to preemptively vomit and run 10 miles. I will NEVER eat that many carbs in one sitting much less in an entire week. Although, it is a franchise, there are only seven other Hash Houses, three in Vegas. Solid wine list too. You will be amazed at their dinner menu. You won't find hipsters here, but that's the point, it's one of those gems hidden in plain sight that can't be obscure enough to be cool. UNR students and locals also get a whopping 20% discount on their food.

Roxy

Eldorado, 4 Star

Roxy at Eldorado seems like a French restaurant but their menu is more like an American steakhouse. They do however have escargot and French onion soup. The best part is the vertical tasting of port which can get you hammered as well as their wine flights. Every restaurant should have wine flights! Don't make the mistake of sitting "outside" by the fountains where people constantly walk by and take photos. The interior is much more cozy and calm. While Eldorado recently went public, as a private company, the Eldorado was one of the best casinos in Reno with some of the best bars, clubs, and restaurants. I truly believe this was the result of the Carano's being personally involved, and they still are. **Gregg Carano** is still the Senior Vice President of Food & Beverage. If you pay close enough attention, you notice the small things he has done that few other major casinos do including a more extensive beer list at the casino bars; higher quality food; outstanding, strong martinis at Roxy; and he used to employ two of the best bartenders in Reno at Cin Cin, **Nicole Barker** and **Annalisa Suarez** before they moved on to The Eddy and Pignic respectively.

The Brewer's Cabinet

475 S Arlington Ave, 3 Star

Again, you would expect mediocre fried food at a brewery but like Brasserie St. James, their food gets as much attention as their brews if not more. Unfortunately, the hipster, bare wall décor gets overdone here creating a sound cave that can cause deafness. In twenty years, hipsters be like, "What? I can't hear anymore. I used to work in a hipster restaurant."

Pho 777

102 E 2nd St, 3 Star

When you're eating in a room-full of East Asians, you know you're eating in an authentic East Asian restaurant. Either that or you could be at McDonalds in China. Pho 777 has this cheap, open San Francisco feel to it, which is good. The food is good, but maybe it's just the ambiance of a room packed full of East Asians. This is authentic Vietnamese food, although I'm not quite sure there is any unauthentic Americanized Vietnamese food out there yet, besides the pork belly bun taco. It used to be in the old Mizpah Hotel building before some fricking nuthole burned the building down, but perhaps fortunate for Pho 777, because the old place was way too small. I always think they should call it Pho 775 for Northern Nevada's area code. Yo, Pho 775, recognize, give a shout out, hey hey!

Men's Club

270 Lake St, 3 Star

They have great sushi here, but that's not the point. The point is, you're eating sushi at a strip club, that's the point. Of course, I think because of health code, they keep the strippers in a separate room, but none-the-less, you're eating sushi at a strip club folks. The sushi actually is in the top 10 percentile in Reno.

Zagol

855 E 4th St, 3 Star

This is an Ethiopian restaurant where everything is served on a spongy pancake called Injera that is so exotic, not even Microsoft Word recognizes what Injera is. Add that to the dictionary. They do not give you utensils and expect you to use the Injera to pick up the meat. It may be a little heavy on the carbs, but here's my trick: I use the same piece of Injera to pick up meat multiple times until it falls apart. Always use your right hand to eat if you want to be culturally correct. I imagine they have utensils for novices. I actually met an Ethiopian in Reno, and she told me that Zagol Americanizes their food to accommodate our weirdo palates. Ethiopian food is spicier, and she said that in larger cities, they actually charge less for the same stuff. None-the-less, it's not like you're going to walk across the street to the other Ethiopian restaurant in town (there is none).

Beto's

575 W 5th St, 3 Star

Do you like Taco Bell? Do you like the fried, macho-super-8-layer chalupaduper with sour cream? Uh go to Taco Bell or whatever fake Mexican restaurant is out there. If you want the real deal, the stuff Mexican mothers cook for their families, the stuff you'll find in Mexico 100 miles away from tourist towns, then go to Beto's. If the place is packed with more hipsters than Mexicans, you can be sure the food is authentic. One of the best parts of this restaurant is their food truck parked outside that is usually open until 3 AM.

Honey Bakery

403 Keystone Ave, 3 Star

This is not a restaurant, but I have to mention it. They make authentic Chinese Bau's here, buns with meat inside. You have to go early if you want the greater selection because later on they only have a few selections left, which is good, because you know they make them fresh. My favorite is the one with curry filling inside!

Crème

18 St Lawrence Ave, 3 Star

Not a big breakfast fan, but if you want awesome crepes filled with ham and cheese and solid quiche, go to Crème. The best crepes I had was actually from a Middle Eastern dude at a crepes stand in Paris. It was filled with ground beef and humongous. I actually only ate there since I like to eat at around 3 PM and none of the restaurants in Paris are open that early.

Asi Es Mi Tierra

1020 S Wells Ave, 3 Star

This is a Mexican/El Salvadoran restaurant with pupusas and empanadas. They also have El Salvadoran beer. The décor is a bit run down, but if you want authentic, this is it. If you think about it, even if you go to El Salvador, you're not going to find authentic El Salvadoran food in a place that looks like Applebee's.

Naan'n'Kabab

2740 S Virginia St, 3 Star

In 2012, readers of both the Reno Gazette-Journal and Reno News & Review voted this place the second best Indian restaurant in Reno. It is the funniest and saddest thing Renoites have ever done. This is a Mediterranean restaurant. Last time I checked, India was not on the Mediterranean coastline. You see, Renoites think these surveys are like high school exams. If you don't know the answer, it is better to guess than leave it blank, but in the case of these surveys, it totally screws everything up when people are guessing what the best places are just based on their names. And that is why you should keep buying my book!

Crawfish Asian Cuisine

1296 Plumb Ln, 3 Star

In Vegas, besides the burger fetish, there are two places where you can get a bag of crawfish and can open them up on a sheet of wax paper, Hot N Juicy Crawfish and Boiling Crab. Hot N Juicy is so popular, they built another restaurant only two blocks away. They also have king crab, lobster, clams, and shrimp. Crawfish Asian is the Reno version which serves crawfish like this as well as a regular Chinese food menu and also a secret Chinese menu only Edward Snowden knows about. Personally, I think secret Chinese menus suck. I know waitresses get sick and tired of having to try to explain esoteric Chinese dishes and sometimes, especially when the dishes are fermented, customers send them back. But seriously, younger Americans are into authentic and esoteric and sometimes challenging cuisines. Chinese restaurants, expose your secret menus! While the main courses here are pricey and worth it, I don't believe the pricey appetizers are worth their price.

Burger Me

6280 Sharlands Ave #101 (on your way to Reno right off I-80), 3 Star

They have hormone, chemical-free beef as well as buffalo and lamb burgers. It may not be as succulent as **Five Guys**, but it's healthier. There's a place called Little Nugget that has this Awful Awful Burger everyone here raves about, but you know what, they're all blacked-out drunk when they eat it, so they should shut up, it's not that great a burger. Carl's Jr. has a natural burger free of antibiotics and grass fed. I know it's kind of like the Nazis opening a spa resort for Communists, but at least for those Commies it's better than a prison camp. You notice I didn't say Jews, because it's still a sensitive subject.

DeLuxe Café (formerly Electric Blue Elephant food truck)

148 West St, 3 Star

Some of the best vegan, gluten-free, dairy-free food you will eat in your life including a hand salad. There should be more salad rolls/wraps/burritos. I used to make my own salad burritos at home, although, I haven't quite figured out how to cram a whole salad in there as tightly as a Cuban cigar.

Laughing Planet Café

650 Tahoe St and 941 N Virginia St, 3 Star

This is pretty much the most hipster restaurant in Reno. First of all, they're from Portland. Yeah, PDX hipster cred. Second, they have kale, quinoa, Korean BBQ, vegan, and gluten-free fare. This is all good stuff, don't get me wrong, but it's just funny when everyone jumps on the same good stuff bandwagon like it's a trend and not just something good for you. You know you're a hipster when you have to pick quinoa out of your beard.

Pignic Pub & Patio

235 Flint St, 3 Star

You've heard of BYOB. This is BYOM, Bring Your Own Meats. Here's how it works. Pay $10, get $10 back in drinks, they provide everything you need to grill and clean up afterwards. Is this not a brilliant idea?! No more asking the waiter where the beef comes from, whether it was grass or grain fed, injected with antibiotics and hormones, or massaged by wallabies in Australia. On top of this, steaks are often half the price when bought from a grocer. How can you not love this idea?

Honorable Mention by Food Category

New American

Some of the best restaurants in Reno are New American. **Gas Lamp** seems Cajun inspired by their name and jambalaya dish but it's more eclectic. They have a creative menu and great cocktails. There's also a local's favorite called **Pinocchio's Bar & Grill** that really isn't what you'd think a bar & grill is. In my opinion, bar & grills are more bar than grill or at least it has substantial bar space. Although, Pinocchio's has a lot of Italian cuisine, it also has a lot of non-Italian cuisine like grilled Cajun chicken, New York Steak, and BBQ baby back ribs. There are two Pinocchio's, one in Reno at its new location on S Virginia St and one in Sparks. **Moxie's** at Caughlin Ranch has average food but what puts this in honorable mention is their fantastic view of Reno. **Bricks** is pricey but worth it and the horrible 70's music. **Sierra Street Kitchen and Cocktails** newly opened next door to Campo, a location that has always been overshadowed by the most popular restaurant in town. **Feast** is a new up-and-comer.

Vegetarian/Vegan

Dandelion's Deli offers both vegan and carnivore food. The **Kitchen at the Great Basin Food Co-op** has fresh, organic vegetarian food. When I was growing up, vegetarian meant a tasteless tofu burger. Today, vegetarian and vegan fare are comparable in taste, flavor, texture, and substance as flesh meals. When I was growing up, vegetarians were elfish waifs with hair falling out. These days, they can be bearded, brawny ogres.

Italian

There are a lot of Italian restaurants in Reno because the early settlers here were Italian and Basque and there was a big New York migration. Most all of them are that old, classic Italian from the hole-in-the-wall to the very upscale and trendy. I bet you they all have fettuccini Alfredo and beef ravioli. Many of them have veal and seafood too.

While I love pasta and Italian food, this is really Americanized Italian food just like Americanized Mexican food and Americanized Chinese. Yes, they eat fettuccini Alfredo in Italy, just as they eat burritos in Mexico and chow mein in China, but why for heck's sake do all these ethnic restaurants all have the same twenty menu items??? Oh, that's right, because 99% of their customers will order the same twenty things, and if they add a new item, chances are, nobody will order it, and it gets spoiled, and they will simply throw it out at a loss or feed it to staff. And that is exactly what happened with beers too. 99% of Americans ordered the same ten beers, and if the bar owner got creative and added something new, chances are, nobody tried it, and it just sat there forever taking up space and wound up skunky.

Let's not blame the restaurants or bars; they were only doing what they could to stay in business. In a business with the highest failure rates, who can really blame them for erring on the side of safety? Fortunately, times have changed and now restaurants and bars that are not innovating are going out of business. For good representations of classic American-Italian food, go to **LaFamiglia, Mario's Portofino, Johnny's Ristorante Italiano,** or **Luciano's** for their tortellini alla papalina.

There are two hidden Italian oddities, oddly close together along East 4th Street. From the outside, **Casale's Half Way Club** looks like a dive bar, but inside they have decent Italian food. **Coney Island Bar** a little east of there is a bar with an Italian restaurant only open on Wednesday nights. Occasionally, they have a big Cioppino feast served family style. An interesting story: back in about 1999 I went inside, because they had a PBR sign outside. This was when PBR was not cool, as cool as a Hamm's if that. They told me they didn't have PBR, they just liked the sign and never took it down. 2012 I go back in for the first time since 1999 guessing that like most dive bars they'd have PBR. Kid you not, they just took it off tap the week before my visit and took the sign down too.

Sushi

Reno has this freakish thing about sushi, and worse, ALL-YOU-CAN-EAT-SUSHI! Are you fricking serious? If you're going to cut corners on food, the heck you want to do it with raw seafood! Seriously? Of course, I do enjoy the inventive, creative, bizarre fried concoctions especially the ones with jalapenos, cream cheese, and cilantro. Why not stick some rib eye meat in there? Why only seafood? The Koreans have gimbap which is sushi but they sometimes use ham. The Hawaiians have sushi with Spam. This is my roll; I call it the Rocky Balboa Roll: rib eye, melted cheddar cheese, caramelized onions, black pepper, olive oil, mushrooms, cream cheese, jalapenos, cilantro, and rice. The Miss Piggy Roll: Prosciutto, soppressata, provolone, maple syrup, sundried tomatoes, shitake mushrooms, olive oil, onions, garlic, basil, black pepper, jalapenos, cilantro, and rice. My greatest invention, however, has to be the salad roll, and you should be able to have this at any restaurant. I hate eating salad in public, because it's messy with big chunks of lettuce dangling out your mouth and salad dressing all over your face. Think about it, salad is like painting your face with salad dressing using a fork and lettuce. So why not roll up tomatoes, cucumbers, lettuce, and salad dressing in seaweed into a tight long roll, cut that up and voila, salad you can conveniently pick up and place into your mouth neatly. In most Asian cultures, you never cut your food at the table, hence no knife and fork. Everything is served in bite-sized pieces.

If you are crazy enough to do all-you-can-eat sushi, you might as well go to **Hiroba**, **Da Joint**, **Ijji's**, **Kitzmo**, **Wasabi**, or **Reef**. Unfortunately, the only time you get to drink sake is at a sushi bar. There is as much to learn about sake as beer or wine. Who knew you could get so many different flavors from rice? Premium sake is divided by how much they polish the rice which gets rid of the outer layer that messes up the flavor. Honjozo is polished a lot. Ginjoshu polished a heck of a lot. Daiginjoshu is polished so much it sometimes can lose over half its original weight. It is also divided by whether distilled alcohol is added. If none is added, then it is Junmai sake. Some say sake is classified as a beer, but it should be its own category, because it is not made like beer although it uses yeast. It also uses mold, yes, sake is made from moldy rice. And you don't add distilled alcohol to beer.

Chinese

I get sick at half of all the Chinese restaurants I go to. Chinese cooks simply have this tradition of letting meat sit out at room temperature all day long, as do ironically many warm-climate nations. But it makes sense, because they all use a lot of seasonings and spices to hide the flavor of meat gone bad for lack of cold temperature. Honorable mention: **Dynasty** and the chain **PF Chang**. **Asian Noodles** has "fondue" style dining. No, you don't dip your egg rolls in a fountain of chocolate. They bring out steaming hot soup and stick it in a hole in the table and you can cook your own raw and fresh food right there. Because the Cantonese were the first to export Chinese cuisine to the world, most people wrongly think all Chinese food is the Cantonese style: spicy, heavy sauces, and mostly rice dishes. It seems almost universal that the further north you travel, the blander, more whole, and minimalist-tasting the food becomes.

Vietnamese

Saigon 88 in Sparks and **Golden Flower** make honorable mention. Golden Flower is open until 3 AM for your late night drunken eating.

Korean

American is slowly making its way through Asian cuisine starting with Chinese, then sushi in the 80's, Thai, Vietnamese, and now Korean. Korean BBQ at the table is all the rage. Reno finally jumped on board with **Ijji 4 Korean Bar-B-Que** which is pretty authentic as far as the American-Korean BBQ experience followed recently by **Siu Korean BBQ** in Sparks both all-you-can-eat. In Korea, however, kalbi is so old generation. The Korean kids today are into spicy chicken grilled and shared at the table called Dak Galbi which is a lot more affordable. Quite possibly the best thing I've ever tasted when they add cheese. The only other Korean place in town is **Hana Garden** in Sparks. This place is not great, but it is a good representation of authentic Korean food with authentic Korean ingredients and authentic Korean cooks and authentic Korean TV shows playing. As with most all foreign cuisine in America, kimchi is dumbed down using fewer spices and garlic, however, I do actually appreciate kimchi with less garlic which leaves your breath funky for several hours. **Bab Café** recently opened which is basically a hipster lunch spot.

In case you didn't know, the Korean government is the first in the world to subsidize their pop culture not only as a profitable global industry but also to market the nation as a brand. Koreans are obsessed with image, and it's no surprise they have more cosmetic surgery per capita than any other nation on Earth. Much of this can be attributed to Japanese Occupation where Koreans were treated as an inferior race and their culture mostly destroyed.

Filipino

Manila Hongkong Kitchen is hidden in an Asian grocery store in Sparks. There is also **Silong** in Sparks. They both serve food cafeteria style. **Café de Manila** in Reno is a regular restaurant with waiters. What is Filipino food? It's a lot like beef or chicken stews with rice and some can be slightly pungent with fermented fish sauce. It's an acquired taste that gets better each time. Of course, no matter how many times I try soft-ripened French cheese, I still gag. I consider Filipino food somewhat bland like English food. There used to be one called ALM Kainan inside of Wienerschnitzel in Sparks, seriously.

Ramen

There's a great foodie movie called *Ramen Girl* starring the deceased Brittany Murphy. It follows an American girl who winds up in Japan and works hard to learn the ancient Japanese art of ramen. Most people assume ordering ramen at a restaurant is like ordering spaghetti at an Italian restaurant, but chef-made ramen is truly an art in Japan. You can find gourmet ramen at **Uchi Ramen**.

Thai

Bangkok Cuisine has two locations and is a Reno favorite. **Lanna Thai Café** also has a culinary school. I've heard good things about **Sawasdee** in Sparks. **SF Kitchen** offers Thai, Vietnamese, and Chinese.

Mexican

Reno has a lot of American-Mexican restaurants with super, fun margaritas and fake Mexican food. Some that are just really good or a bit more authentic are **Arroyo**, **Si Amigo**, **El Adobe**, **Bertha Mirandas**, **Cantina Los Tres Hombres**, **Los Compadres**, **Macho Tequila**, **Cantina Hussong's** (a small chain), **Costa Vida Fresh Mexican Grill** (a chain)**, Chipotle** (a big healthy chain)**,** or **Miguel's**. While there are no Cuban restaurants in Reno, **Carniceria La Chiquita** has the Torta Cubana, a Frankenstein transmutation including bacon, ham, Milanesa, cheese, and a hot dog!

Pupusas

Just because I love pupusas, I'm listing all the places in town that have good pupusas: **Cantina, Speedy Burrito, Asi Es Mi Tierra, Restaurante Yesenia, El Rincon, Bistro Habanero, Casa de Oro, Mi Querido Pulgarcito, El Paisano Taqueria y Pupuseria** (both Reno and Sparks) and **Los Cuatro Vientos** (the four winds).

Indian

I'd stick with all vegetarian at an Indian restaurant. Besides Chinese and some Mexican food trucks, I also tend to get sick at Indian restaurants. I don't know why they have all-you-can-eat. Would Gandhi approve of that? Or for that matter Deepak Chopra? It's paradoxical like an Amish-themed Vegas casino. **India Kabob & Curry** is popular in Reno and greets you with a creepy-as-hell mannequin. I prefer **Flavors of India** which recently changed ownership and offers less sauce, more flavor, and higher prices. **Thali Reno** is a vegetarian Indian restaurant that recently opened next door to the **West St Wine Bar** and you can eat your meals at the wine bar.

BBQ

For a place that has the Sparks Nugget Rib Cook-Off our BBQ scene was lacking for a while, but that has changed recently. **Men Wielding Fire,** chain **Dickey's, Brothers, CBQ** in Sparks, and **BJ's Nevada BBQ** in Sparks (not to be confused with BJ Brewery) are five solid BBQ joints. Most every other place gives you scrap meat with a couple actual rib bones here and there, and the scrap meat is overcooked and inedible. At the risk of discrediting myself but for sake of honesty, I'll add **Boston Market**'s BBQ ribs.

Diners

Okay, fine, if you must get greasy diner food, you might as well pretend you're back in the 50's and go to chain **Mel's Diner** at Sands or Damonte Ranch and chain **Johnny Rocket's** in the Grand Sierra. Chain **Black Bear Diner** is also pretty decent minus the 50's decor. (For sake of nostalgia about nostalgic diners, Vonz Diner in Golden Valley and Joe's Diner on S Virginia recently closed.)

All-You-Can-Eat Buffets

Uh no. I get hives just walking by them. The only exception is perhaps if I was preparing for the Tour de France and needed an inexpensive 3,000 calorie meal. As much as I like eclectic fare, the temptation to overeat to stretch your dollar outweighs the diversity of tastes. The exception is the Vegas all-you-can-eat buffets which offer gourmet treats. They even have an all-you-can-eat, all-day-long option. Only in Vegas. Think of Vegas as that human colony in the *Wall-E* movie. The modern American mentality is to push everything to their natural conclusions which is the definition of insanity. Whether you like it or not, the Goldilocks Principle applies to humans as well as planets. We exist in a very small range that is healthy for us, just as we can only see a very small range of the electromagnetic spectrum, and exposure to certain wavelengths can harm and kill us. So what is the point of pushing ourselves outside this range? Happiness is found within the range. Profiteering and self-destruction can be found outside that range. Vegas is all-you-can-do, but as with all-you-can-eat buffets, to enjoy yourself, you don't have to push yourself to the breaking point to have fun.

Steak

At **Harrah's Steakhouse** I can't get enough of watching a chef come out of the kitchen to prepare Steak Diane for you. There are some classic steak places in Reno: **Rapscallion's**, **Vista Grille,** and relatively inexpensive chain **Ruby River** if you can stand incessant country music. The reason I don't include many steakhouses among the best restaurants in Reno is because they're mostly over-priced, old-fashioned, over-rated, boring, lack innovation, and/or do not serve grass-fed, hormone-free cows. Whenever I travel, I always to try find a steak place that serves grass-fed, hormone-free steaks, because it's just not a thing in Reno yet. I honestly believe Reno is ready for a $50 grass-fed, hormone-free steak.

Greek

Blue Plate, **Nick's Greek Deli**, **Naan'n'Kabob**, and **Spiro's Bar & Grill** in Sparks. All solid Greek, although Naan'n'Kabob's "Awesome Dude" baklava on top of their Akbar Mashdi' ice cream takes the baklava. Opa's closed which was famous for their commercials featuring an old Greek dude dancing and yelling "opa."

Mediterranean

The Mediterranean has arrived in Reno with a bunch of brand new restaurants: **Hummus, Suri's Mediterranean, Zayna Flavors of Morocco,** and **Wrap It Up** (which has Shawarma – meat slices piled on a pole and cut off). Newly opened **Shawarmageddon** gets credit for a great name. Quite possibly the coolest, funkiest, smallest restaurant in Reno.

Cajun/Southern/Soul

Gas Lamp is Cajun inspired. **M&M's Southern Café** (no relation to the candy which is exploring all sorts of new flavors) in Sparks has southern-style soul food.

Pizza

Brugo's, Blind Onion, and **Blue Moon** are pretty good and chain **Grimaldi's** in Sparks has a good, thin crust with a very bizarre dining room that looks like a fancy Italian restaurant. **True New York Pizza** in Sparks is New York style but not the soft, soggy New York style I like. There are actually two types of New York style pizza. In Little Italy, New York Style pizza means a thicker, crunchier crust with better ingredients like Lombardi's baked in a coal oven. Everywhere in Midtown Manhattan you'll find cheap pizza-by-the-slice joints often owned by Middle Eastern immigrants. The slices are huge but extremely thin and floppy, and some New Yorkers even fold it in half after padding the grease off with a napkin. I prefer the cheap Midtown Manhattan style you can find all over Vegas but nowhere in Reno. **Extreme Pizza** is a chain from California but none-the-less a quality chain. The area finally gets a Chicago-style pizza with **Taste of Chicago** which used to be a hot dog cart. For late night, drunk eating, **Hidden Pizza** on the 2nd floor of the Eldorado across Brew Brothers has edible-when-drunk thin-crust pizza by the slice. Once you walk up the stairs from the Roxy, you think you're entering Silver Legacy, but both Brew Brothers and Hidden Pizza are still part of Eldorado.

Burgers

Burgers are a big thing these days with gourmet, near-gourmet, and higher priced fast food burgers cropping up all over Vegas and America. The fad has arrived in Reno with **Five Guys** which I believe has the best fast food burger around. I like the way they use local farms for their French fries. FYI, according to Wikipedia, ground beef is comprised of skeletal, connective, and peripheral nerve tissue and blood vessels. **Fuddrucker's** has the next best tasting burgers around. Little Nugget's Awful Awful is overrated overrated. Clary's used to have these stuffed burgers you could fill with almost anything. I had a peanut butter-filled burger one night, and the bartender thought I was high off my ass. You can find **Habit**

Burger at Circus Circus. We also have **Steak 'n Shake**, but their burgers are bland and contrary to the name, do not use steak meat. **Whole Foods** has a good burger that does not use antibiotics or growth hormones. It takes a while to cook, so you should order it first and then go shopping.

Hot Dogs/Sausages

Mellow Fellow across the baseball stadium has exotic sausages like elk with apple pear, buffalo with chipotle, venison with blueberry, and pheasant with cognac, all nitrate-free. A truly hidden gem is **CJ's Hot Dog** stand usually found on Virginia Street across from the Eldorado. In addition to wild game dogs, he has a hot dog with chow mein and Japanese mayonnaise as well as a Korean dog (that is NOT made out of real dogs). **Bam!dog** recently opened and capitalizes on the exotic topping hot dogs. Japadog in Vancouver BC has perhaps the world's best hot dog topped with Japanese mayo (mayo is huge in Japan), seaweed, noodle and kimchi. Again, at the risk of my credibility, I'm going to mention **Maverick** gas station's Cheddarwurst Wrap and Bahama Mama Wrap. Think of **Maverick** as the Disneyland of gas station stores. There is a new one at N. McCarran Bl and Sutro St.

Philly Cheesesteaks/Subs

There is a place in Reno and one in Sparks called Philadelphia Cheesesteak, but having lived in Philadelphia, they ain't true Philly Cheesesteak. FYI, Kraft cheese whiz is only a modern, disgusting addition to the cheesesteak. Cheez Whiz has 28 ingredients, only one of which is cheese. **Yellow Submarine** in Sparks is a local favorite. Chain **Port of Subs** opened its first store in Sparks in 1972 and now they have franchises throughout the west, a true local success story. Unlike other sub places, they use fresh ingredients they slice on the spot like an old New York deli. Pretty hipster for 1972. We used to have Schlotsky's which I really liked. **Gramma Ginna's** inside Scheels in Sparks has elk meat.

Deli's

Yosh's Deli and **Pedalers Deli** are local favorites. I've never been to them since I'm not much of a sandwich guy. Although, I get excited about peanut butter and jelly sandwiches at Whole Foods. I wish someone would make a damn gourmet bologna sandwich! A notable new addition is **Bazaar Russian Store European Deli and Café** which specializes in Eastern European groceries and including most importantly beer! It's almost a reincarnation of Moscow Deli.

New York Style Deli's

If you want a good old Reuben or pastrami on rye, go to **Paisan's Old World Deli, Michael's, Newman's,** or the chain **Gandolfo's**. **Manhattan Deli** inside the Atlantis has a lot of Jewish food like bagels and lox, gefilte fish, knishes, blintzes, latke, matzo ball soup, and challah bread. They also have Middle Eastern foods for sale. It's probably because John Farahi who runs the place is an Iranian Jew. Of course, what is Jewish food? Much like Malaysian food, it's really a fusion of different cultures. In the case of Jews, since they moved around so much, they picked up a lot of their food culture from the Middle East, Russia, and Germany. If the Jews had moved to China, there would be bagel and chow mein.

Morning and Lunch Restaurants

I don't eat breakfast or lunch, because I usually don't eat until at least 3 PM, but I have heard about some great morning and lunch restaurants: **Squeeze Inn, Daughter's Cafe, Rose's, Peg's Glorified Eggs, Dish Cafe,** and **Wet Hen Cafe**. **Two Chicks** used to be a food truck. There's also the chain **Einstein's Bagels** that has thankfully thin bagels for all you carbaphobes. Some places will cut out the middle slice of the bagel for you. It's like just eating muffin tops.

Food Trucks

Food trucks are simply awesome. They've been around forever, mostly Mexican ones, but there's a new fad involving all sorts of eclectic food. The first true pioneer in inventive, gourmet food trucks was Kogi BBQ in Los Angeles which had Korean tacos and was the first to use Twitter to update customers on its location. **Kenji's** has Korean bulgogi tacos, **DishTruck** has sandwiches, and **Burger Me** has hormone-free, antibiotic-free burgers including a lamb burger. DishTruck has carnitas tacos that would beat any Mexican taco truck if only they put more hot sauce on it. The owners of Gourmelt food truck replaced their truck with **Two Chicks** restaurant in Midtown.

Chains

Okay, I'm not fanatically anti-corporate, anti-chain. I've listed a few already, but I will give **BJ's Brewery** special mention as a pretty nice chain with good microbrews and great food for a brewery which usually serves average fried stuff. It has what I'd call 00's chain décor: coffee colors everywhere, open, airy, spacious, high ceilings, and upscale. If it were the 00's, people would be lining up for this place in their baggy 2XL shirts, pleated khaki pants and loafers. **Buffalo Wild Wings** is also a pretty snazzy sports bar.

Late Night Restaurants

Golden Flower is open until 3 AM and **Hong Kong Diner** is open until 3:30 AM. Hong Kong Diner is basically subpar Chinese junk food while Golden Flower has a nice mix of Chinese and Vietnamese.

24-Hour Restaurants

In addition to 24-hour bars and casinos, Reno also has 24-hour restaurants. Most large casinos have 24-hour restaurants. **Gold'n'Silver** is a decent old-fashioned American diner with nice seafood specials. Food can be a little inconsistent depending on the chef de la nuit. **Taqueria La Michoacana** is 24-hours and has very authentic, cheap Mexican food although I sometimes get sick here. **Archie's, Corkscroo**, and **Bully's** have 24-hour regular bar and grill stuff. **Spiro's** in Sparks is also a 24-hour bar and grill but it also has Greek food.

Monte Cristo

There have been articles about each state's signature food and Nevada either has none or it's something obscure and untrue. Perhaps sushi should be our signature food, perhaps the prime rib, but I would also offer the Monte Cristo, a classic casino diner dish, basically a deep-fried grilled ham-and-cheese sandwich. I have heard **Purple Parrot** diner at the Atlantis makes a good one. **Still Rollin** food truck turns sandwiches into egg rolls and has a Monte Cristo egg roll.

Solo Diner Restaurants

If for whatever reason you don't have a dining companion but still want to enjoy excellent food in Reno, some restaurants are perfect for solo dining while others make you feel like a real loner loser. The following is a list of restaurants that I find particularly friendly toward loner loser - I mean solo dining if you don't mind dining at a bar. The best place is a restaurant with a separate bar from the main dining area. Figure it out restaurants! Lots of loners in the world today!

Restaurants with a medium to large bar completely separated from the dining area:

LuLou's (lounge), **CHI, Charlie Palmer** (lounge), **Brick's, Twisted Fork, Louis' Basque Corner,** and **Cin Cin. Cin Cin** is a lounge with a small bar where you can have **La Strada** food, and when they're closed Wednesday and Thursday, you can have **Prime Rib Grill** food.

Restaurants with medium to large bars somewhat separated from the dining area:

Bistro 7, Old Granite, Brewer's Cabinet, PF Chang

Wild River Grille has the **River Room** next door along Virginia that is less busy and a long bar open to the dining area behind. **Stone House** has a small bar that is open to the dining area, but a small part of the dining area so it doesn't look too bad dining solo there. There are two bars at **Brasserie St. James** where you can eat at the bar but both are open to the dining areas and often packed with people not eating. **Roundabout** has a nice long bar. Most sushi places you can sit at the bar and most people will not notice that you are by yourself so long as you are sitting next to at least one person.

Keep in mind, casinos are a great place for solo diners to grab a bite, because people will just assume you're one of those convention or business people just visiting town without your spouse or date in town.

Most all microbreweries, bar & grills, and sports bar have large bars where you can grab a bite solo.

Notable Restaurants No Longer Here

This section is for old locals, a little cruise down memory lane in your 1987 Buick Regal:

Hooter's

3655 S Virginia St

People think Hooter's is this sexist, anachronistic, sleazeball restaurant, and it is, and that's why it does so well. Hello? In *Undercover Boss*, they had a Hooter's CEO get all disturbed that women didn't like Hooter's, and I'm thinking, well shit dude if you want to cover up your staff and hire dudes, why not just rename the place Applebee's?

Davo's

777 E 4th St

Location, location, location. It was in the parking lot of a roach motel called Rancho 777. I've seen a postcard of the motel back in the day, and yeah, back in the day, it looked like a really nice place with super big cars in the parking lot. I'll never forget when the owner and chef came out to greet the table, I handed him the bill and he politely placed it back down on the table and asked if we enjoyed our meal. Embarrassing! Oh, it was an Italian restaurant back when it was okay to stuff your face with carbs slathered with thick, creamy 500 calories of Alfredo sauce.

Columbo's

down by the river

No, not after it moved but before, by the river. I never went here, but hear it was the place to go and had great evening entertainment. I was basically too poor to afford this place back then. I'd walk by and lick the window.

Tony's Pizza of New York

1901 Silverada Blvd Ste 18

Tony's was the real deal and the dude was from New York.

Tony Roma's

Sands

Speaking of Tony. Actually Reno used to have great ribs. It was called Tony Roma's. I know it's a big corporate franchise, but still, I loved going there, and back then big corporate franchises and baggy 2XL shirts you could fit a German Shepherd inside were cool, and you could choose what sauces to put on your meat.

Deux Gros Nez

249 California Ave

Some bicycle racing fanatic dreamed up this café and restaurant which was hipster before hipster. It had a sister restaurant called Pneumatic Diner at 501 W 1st St which also closed. Deux Gros Nez FYI means two big noses in French. There's a book called, *Slaying the Badger* about the epic 1986 Tour de France battle between American neophyte Greg LeMond and old French cycling legend Bernard Hinault. Keep in mind, no American had ever won the Tour de France. This is before Lance Armstrong Le Grand Doper. Also keep in mind, the Tour de France is like the Super Bowl and the two were on the SAME team. The previous year, Hinault had promised that he would help LeMond win the Tour after LeMond helped him. This was Joe Montana and Steve Young times a billion. In fact, in one stage, LeMond could have beaten Hinault but was directed to hold back for his team leader given misinformation that Hinault was a lot closer behind than he really was. In 1986, instead of chasing down breaks and protecting LeMond's wheel, Hinault continually attacked, extending his lead over LeMond until LeMond finally destroyed him on Stage 17. I always thought this would make a great movie. It had everything: foreign intrigue, an innocent and talented hero, betrayal, sports, and patriotism. A fine example of reality being better than fiction. LeMond will always be in my mind the greatest cyclist and arguably the fastest human on a bicycle, arguably without drug enhancements which is a whole other story.

Blue Heron

1091 S. Virginia St

Reno's old vegetarian hippie restaurant

Famous Murphy's

3127 S Virginia St

Can someone please tell me why they closed? This was Reno's great beloved, upscale, classic, warm, Irish restaurant. It was the kind of place lawyers would hang out after work talking about hammering out corrupt development deals. During the flood of 1997, they provided free food to volunteers.

Adele's

425 S Virginia St

Back in the day, I really couldn't afford places like this and always felt out of place in here. I mean seriously, the waiter had a nicer car than I did. It was so damn fancy and intimidating. It had seafood, steaks, and pasta, and set the bar for fine dining in Reno. They closed this location and remain open in Carson City. You ever notice how the nicer the restaurant the longer the waiter's apron? I mean seriously, at the most expensive places, the waiters are practically tripping over their aprons. And you notice how waiters change with the price of the meal. You start with old women at the low end, then you move to young dudes and young average-looking women, then as the price moves up, the women get hotter and hotter, and then at the very top, no, you don't get supermodels, you get OLD MEN!

Liberty Belle

Where the Reno-Sparks Convention Center is now

These guys are funny. They refused to sell to the City of Reno which built a huge ass convention center AROUND them. It was like a Star Wars brand new, state-of-the-art architecture looking facility, and stuck right in front of it like a sore ironic thumb was this Western-looking, old restaurant with wagons on the roof and vintage slot machines inside. Fricking awesome, but then they sold and the City of Reno, instead of enshrining the place and turning it into a slot machine museum, demolished it! Damn City of Reno! Right now, you can go to Harrah's on Lake Street and stuck in the middle of Harrah's is Santa Fe Basque Restaurant and hotel. They refused to sell too but decided to stick around.

Midtowne Market

121 Vesta St

I'll never understand why this place closed either. This was a restaurant, bar, espresso café, bakery, cigar bar, and wine store all wrapped into one. They were so popular, and it was so trendy when Reno was so backwards and crusty, old-fashioned. Midtowne was so *Sex and The City*, so cosmo, so hip, so cool!!! You could just imagine Samantha at the bar and some cheesy UNR dude all creeping up on her.

Kyoto

915 W Moana Ln

Unlike most all the sushi places in Reno, Kyoto had other great Japanese food. And I mean, come on, this was like 1995 Reno when people thought Japanese food was just sushi and still had ill feelings about Pearl Harbor. **Wasabi** at the Summit actually reminds me a bit of Kyoto.

Benihana Japanese Steakhouse

210 N Sierra St

I used to know a hot waitress here called Ashley whom I creeped on for a while following her from Mel's Diner to Benihana to Ichiban's, and then at Ichiban's I wound up dating some other waitress who happened to be her friend and ex-roommate. Then Ashley moved to Peru or Chile or something and wound up marrying some dude there. Seriously? Benihana was Reno's teppanyaki place before Ichiban's. There's nothing like a crazed Japanese teppanyaki chef who either huffs paint or takes psychedelics with speed, playing with sharp knives at lightning speed, insulting and throwing food at perplexed white folk.

EJ's Jazz Café

17 S Virginia St

Although the place was cramped, narrow, the musical acoustics sucked, and the food was so spicy hot you'd sweat in the middle of winter, it had a great vibe, it was the only place to listen to good jazz, and the owners would actually walk around and meet and greet and give you the impression they loved the place and they loved the food and music and wanted to share that love with you.

Krispy Kreme

5050 Kietzke Ln

You simply have not had a donut if you have never had a Krispy Kreme. These were very light, airy, toasty donuts with a nice sugary glazing. Because they did not have that typical donut heavy cakey feel, you could eat a half dozen easily and get a sugar coma. I think the chain in Reno did well enough to survive, but it was probably their corporate offices that expanded too fast and decided to cut back.

Fin Fish

Grand Sierra

Reno's only decent seafood restaurant in a very trendy room with wood logs dangling from the wall creating a false wall.

Big Apple Pizza

720 Baring Blvd, Sparks

Along with the old Tony's, these guys had the real deal, true New York-style pizza. Everyone used to bitch about how much the pizzas cost, but it was the real deal not Dominoes! For $9.99 do you honestly think you're getting authentic, quality ingredients?

Sezmu

670 Mount Rose St

Sez who? This used to be my favorite restaurant in Reno. Exceptional, innovative food, AND exceptional wine list, AND sustainable restaurant, AND they once had a great waitress/sommelier, Amelia.

Skyline Café

3005 Skyline Bl

Duck ravioli. Duck ravioli. Duck ravioli. LaVecchia restaurant now occupies this place after being thrown out of their original location at Virginia and Moana. It was located in the old Southwest which used to be old Reno wealth before money moved further south outside the McCarran Loop.

Theory

18 St. Lawrence St, 4 Star

These days I guess it's cool to have startlingly bizarre bar/restaurant names (e.g., Our Bar, Death & Taxes, Reno Public House, Bowl) or grossly generic, obscurely traditional, or just plain weird. None-the-less, beside the odd name, Theory got just about everything right from the décor to both a large bar for single diners and a small bar in back where you get to watch the cooks. Their attention to detail was commendable, and their staff had an unmatched knowledge of their dishes. Their food was all hormone-free and grass-fed. The décor was elegant and sophisticated without being over-the-top 90's cosmopolitan (i.e., *Sex and the City*). The food was eclectic including sushi! Perhaps they were a victim of the Great Recession where there were insufficient Renoites available to pay high prices for quality food.

Food Trends That Need to Live or Die

Ghettoizing fancy food (e.g., Duck Confit sliders, Kobe burgers, Osso Bucco tacos, lobster ravioli, scallop pizza, Korobuta hot dogs, Chilean Sea Bass fish fingers, Roquefort Truffle mac-n-cheese): If I had Kobe steaks like every week, I would be curious what a Kobe beef burger tastes like, but in a town when you can't even get Kobe steaks I have no intention whatsoever of eating a Kobe burger. It's kind of like having a Lafite Rothschild wine cooler or mixing 23-year-old Pappy bourbon with coke (I actually dared someone to do this, and he did).

Small menus: I'm not hot about a menu with four entrée options, but I'd be seriously concerned about freshness with a menu with thirty entrée options, so something in between like seven and ten is perfect.

Exotic meat: American cuisine is one of the most diverse in the world; however, what is not diverse is our over-reliance on beef, chicken, and pork. So we get chicken chow mein, chicken Parmesan, chicken curry, chicken tacos, chicken pizza. Diversification of meat would not only be better for our environment, but it would be better for our health. Not only should we eat more lamb, buffalo, elk, wild boar, as well as more diverse fish species, but we should eat more organs and insects. If predators consider eating the liver a sign of dominance and superiority, then why shouldn't we?

Molecular gastronomy: This is the art/science of reducing food to its molecular level so many times you wind up eating foam. Is cotton candy molecular gastronomy? This trend hasn't hit Reno yet, so come visit and we'll decide. I wouldn't mind if you reduced a filet mignon to a dollop of foam, so long as you put that dollop of filet mignon foam on an entire rib eye steak, but don't stick it on a friggin cracker and charge me $30.

Sous-vide: This is the art/science of sealing food in plastic bags and bathing them in water to cook them. Again, this trend hasn't hit Reno.

Vertical presentation (i.e., piling food up vertically): Besides the tendency for the food to get cold faster, who cares?

Squeeze bottle sauces (i.e., sauces squeezed out of bottles to look like Jackson Pollock paintings): It's a bit overdone. How about the chef dips his hand in sauce and makes a hand print on the dish? Or crime scene presentation? Take a plastic bag of sauce, shoot a bullet through it and make it splatter on the plate creating a fine sauce mist.

Organic and local food: This trend should never, ever go away, however, just because it's organic doesn't mean it should taste bland and inferior. Don't put a thin slice of cheese on an elk burger on a wheat bun thinking people eat elk burgers for their health. Well, yes, but that doesn't mean I want it on a rice cracker with green tea paste.

Pop-up restaurants: This trend involves some chef taking over an existing restaurant and either cooking his own stuff concurrently with the existing chefs or just taking over the entire restaurant for the night. This hasn't hit Reno, as far as I know, but I think it's a cool idea, especially when they take over a boring restaurant. Who loses?

Food trucks: In nature, organisms that are mobile and adapt quicker often beat organisms that are stuck in one location and slow to adapt. Food trucks are a step forward in culinary evolution. If you don't believe in evolution, then God created food trucks. What scientist can really argue with the exquisitely complex and perfect food truck menus that could only be the result of divine intervention?

Guerrilla Dinners: Note, this is not a gorilla dinner for gorillas or eating them. Like its namesake, guerrilla marketing and warfare, it is unconventional, small-scale dining. You pay a chef to cook a prix fixe dinner just like you were at a restaurant, but it's often in someone's home with several to dozens of guests. It's underground so they don't get food inspectors and tax collectors up their ying-yang. I've attended one in Reno and that's all I'm saying. This needs to stay.

Mealsharing.com: It hasn't hit Reno yet, but this is a great way to network with no pressure. You can either cook a meal and offer it to strangers or be a stranger and bring a bottle of wine in exchange for a great, home-cooked meal.

What are some Good Places to Buy Fresh Food?

If you're the weirdo type to buy food ingredients and cook them up at home, I would recommend **Natural Grocers**, a new chain that is free of the Whole Foods midday yoga pants mafia. **Great Basin Community Food Co-op** is good but a bit pricey. If you think food co-ops are some Communist hippie concoction, you're probably right, but hey, if they can provide better fresh, natural food than for-profit corporate grocers, who cares right? **Trader Joe's** of course is a good natural, whole food place and yes, I guess there's **Whole Foods, Inc.** **Napa Sonoma** is also a good small gourmet grocer. **Wedge – A Cheese Shop** has fine cheeses and charcuterie (prepared meats like pâtés and prosciutto). **Blue Ribbon Meat Co.** in Sparks and **Sierra Meat & Seafood** in Reno are great butcher shops and meat distributors. **Wolf Pack Meats** operated by the University is a great butcher shop. **Sierra Gold Seafood Market** recently opened and provides the best fresh seafood in town. **Asian Market** in Sparks has a surprising seafood selection. **Butcher Boys** was a popular butcher shop in Sparks, now open in Reno.

Marketon (formerly King Ranch) on Wells is the place to go for a wide selection of Mexican food. There are several Korean and Asian markets around mostly in Sparks. There's stuff there you don't even know if it has eukaryotic or prokaryotic cells. **Bazaar Russian Store European Deli and Café** specializes in Eastern European groceries and beer.

Food Stores no Longer Here

There were also three great food places here that closed: Blue Bounty a gourmet grocer and The Market on South Virginia formerly European Market. Everyone bitched about the prices at Blue Bounty, but seriously, it had great, quality meats and seafood. There was also a great Russian grocer called Moscow Deli that sold Russian and Eastern European beers. They had awesome Pirozhki's (pastries filled with meat). They also had Kinder chocolate eggs with little toys inside which are now outlawed in America.

Where to Party

First of all, if you want to find out what's going on in Reno, there are a few good resources:

www.visitrenotahoe.com/reno-tahoe/what-to-do/events

There was a great app Dibbs, but it went out of business. **www.ediblerenotahoe.com/events** is based on the local magazine, *Edible Reno-Tahoe*. **Reno News & Review**, our independent weekly newspaper also has a good listing of events. You can find it at a number of bars and restaurants downtown and Midtown as well as online. **Reno-Tahoe Tonight** is a large pocket size magazine that has a lot of cool local articles.

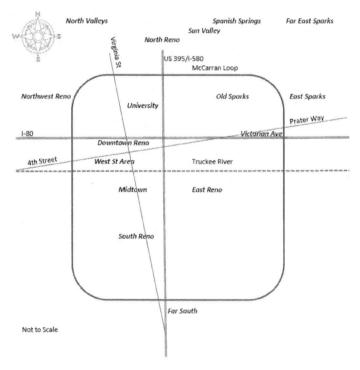

FYI, US 395 in Reno is now called I-580. Nobody knows, and nobody cares.

Unlike restaurants, you don't just hit one bar for the evening; hence, I have listed the bars under party areas. The ideal party area should have at least four bars within walking distance so you don't have to drive around and risk a DUI. These days, obscure, hidden hipster party areas are popping up in poorer parts of town designed to evade tourists and suburban "party commuters".

One thing to keep in mind if you are visiting Reno is to plan it in concurrence with one of several themed bar crawls. (We have monthly daytime bar and wine crawls, but they're nowhere as fun as the nighttime crawls.) The biggest one by far is the Santa Crawl where almost every bar downtown is packed with Santa and other Christmas theme costumes. Downtown Reno is perhaps the ideal bar crawl city because of the density of bars and the casinos where you can safely people watch and mingle. San Diego has a dense nightlife district (the Gaslamp), and I have been on a costume bar crawl there, but I think there are way too many tourists who don't dress up. In Reno, there's a sufficient number of locals who dress up to basically take over downtown. Also, keep in mind, the point of a costume bar crawl is not to drink at every bar. Long lines will drive you nuts. The point is people watching and mingling, so drink beforehand, hide a flask, or get a drink at bars that are not on the bar crawl map. Also, as with most any night, if there's a long line, a lot of clubs have security that will let you bypass the line with a discreet $10 to $20 fee depending on the length of the line and if there is any cover. The organizers of most of the bar crawls recently opened their own bar as the staging area for all their bar crawls aptly named **Headquarters Bar.**

Reno is also experiencing a surge of craft breweries and spirits distilleries. Many have tasting rooms during the day. One great way of checking them all out is the **Reno Tahoe Brewery Tour** (Reno-tahoebrewerytour.com) which will shuttle you around to each venue. They also do a Dive Bar Tour and Virginia City Tour. The last stop of the Dive Bar tour is LabCorps, our local blood testing clinic.

Silver Legacy, Eldorado, and Circus Circus (Downtown Reno)

The Silver Legacy, Eldorado, and Circus Circus are now all owned under the same corporate entity after Eldorado merged with MTR Gaming Group and went public on NASDAQ as ERI trading at around $5 and is now over $30. Gary Carano is Chairman and CEO. A long time ago, Reno had Reno Live, a huge nightclub complex divided into genres with separate rooms for Top 40, hip hop, country, and electronica in the basement. Silverado (as I factitiously call it) has basically recreated Reno Live with **Brew Brothers** doing rock cover bands and a Top 40 DJ later (what I call middle-aged DJ music), **Aura** doing hip hop, **NoVi** doing country, **Rum Bullions** doing rock cover bands, and **El Jefe** doing Latin and middle-aged DJ music.

Brew Brothers

2nd Floor Eldorado

During the day, it's a microbrewery restaurant with mediocre fried shit, but at night, it turns into a very popular club with live bands and DJ's. There's a good mix of tourists, college coeds, and local 20-somethings. Security tells me they get a 50/50 mix of Nevada and California ID's. The best part is "Pickup Row", a walkway from Brew Brothers, between slot machines, to the restrooms and Hidden Pizza. If women are sitting around here, men will descend on them like vultures. Oh, and BTW, the floor is designed to bounce. The place basically sits on a bridge over 4th Street connecting Eldorado and Silver Legacy. For the longest time I never realized this. They have live-band karaoke on Mondays which is exactly what it says. You sing karaoke with a live band backing you up. A professional singer also backs you up in case you start murdering your song. They have flip cup college nights on Thursday where you can pay $7 and drink free draft beer or $10 any house spirit from 10 PM to midnight. Besides **Waldorf**, the only happening place on a Thursday night.

NoVi

2nd Floor Eldorado

Formerly Bubinga, NoVi now has a stage sometimes with live bands and for now, just country bands and happy hour until 11 PM. No cover. FYI, NoVi stands for North Virginia. A DJ comes on with more eclectic music later in the night. Perhaps the only time you'll witness befuddled cowboys watching women twerk on the dancefloor.

Aura

1st Floor Silver Legacy

Aura usually has a $5 cover and hit-or-miss with a lot of tourists. They have a couple go-go dancers. Drinks are a little pricy. Whether you like it or not, certain races gravitate toward certain types of music. For that reason, you might notice that Brew Bros is mostly white with a few Latinos, Asian, and black people; Aura has a lot of black people and Asians; and then NoVi is almost exclusively white.

Rum Bullion's

2nd Floor Silver Legacy

Rum Bullions used to have corny dueling pianos, which is not so corny after a few margaritas. They have live cover band music now trying to mimic the success of Brew Bros. Who can blame them? Not as popular without the dueling pianos. Beers are also pricey.

Roxy Bar & Lounge

2nd Floor Eldorado

Bistro Roxy has a lot of upscale, old folk, but occasionally, younger people. The bar is too small though, and the lounge area gets filled pretty quickly. Great place to bring a date though. A DJ spins on Friday and Saturday nights, and the crowd gets considerably younger. Perhaps the only time you'll witness befuddled old folk watching young women twerk on the dancefloor.

Most of these clubs close around 2 or 3 AM. Of course, this is Friday and Saturday nights. On Thursday nights, notoriously known as college night here and elsewhere, a few bars are packed with college coeds with absolutely no intention whatsoever of going to their two Friday classes.

West Street (Downtown Reno)

The local scene, without doubt, is the southwest corner of downtown. I call it "West Street." Within this magnificent 3x2.5 block nightlife district are 15 eateries/restaurants including: Campo, Sierra Street Kitchen and Cocktails, Roundabout, Liberty Food & Wine, Silver Peak brewery, Thai Corner Café, Noble Pie Parlor Pizza, Thali Reno, DeLuxe Café, Siri's diner, and the Little Nugget's diner. Some of these places are hybrid bar/restaurants. There are 18 bars/clubs including: Ole Bridge, the Jungle, Waterfall (expanded), West St Wine Bar, W 2nd St Bar, Tonic, Rock Bar (concert hall), The Rack, Imperial, 1Up, Blind Dog Tavern, Our Bar, Sierra Tap House, 5 Star, 3rd Street Bar, and Little Nugget bar.

The Rack

111 N Virginia

For now, the Rack is the most popular nightclub in Reno. You can argue that LEX has more people, but because the LEX is so large, if you put a packed crowd from the Rack into the LEX, it would look dead. I also believe we're seeing the twilight of Vegas mega-clubs and the advent of boutique, smaller clubs which is more like Rack. I used to think Vegas mega-clubs were cool at first, but the huge covers, long waits, and then constant standing around in huge crowds gets old after a while. In my opinion, the Rack does everything right with a large bar area and ample seating either at the back of the bar or on sofas behind the bar or a few tables in back. Heck, you can also just go sit at the bowling couches. Yes, there are a few bowling lanes. The only problems I have is that the men's room is relatively small for a packed club with two urinals and a toilet. They should also have a list of all the beers they have in cans available at the bar and not just in the food menu. The music is house, hip hop, and middle-aged DJ.

Imperial

150 N Arlington Ave

Imperial is a large bar with two pool tables and a big center, island bar and is sometimes packed with college kids on Wednesday, Friday and Saturday nights, especially the Greek variety (frat and sorority). Its popularity rises and falls every couple years. Right now, it's down except on Wednesday. The college crowd has anointed **Our Bar** as the place to be the last few years. I personally think the Greek society decides which bars are cool at the beginning of each school year. I used to have my little Rat Pack here owning the pool tables, but that little family has since dissipated which often happens in Reno. I liked to think of myself as Dean Martin not Don Rickles. They also serve food here until about 11 PM and close around 3 AM. The time to find women here is between 11 PM and midnight. I honestly have no idea why that window of time. One of the hidden food gems is their mac'n'cheese where you can add anything they put on their pizzas (e.g., cilantro, mushroom, garlic, anchovies, spinach, prosciutto).

West Street Wine Bar

148 West St

This was the first real wine bar in Reno, and the owner has done a great job stocking eclectic, independent, and smaller vineyards. You won't find a Rombauer Chard or Mondavi Cab here. It has a very sophisticated mellow feel, and I honestly wish it were twice as big with twice as many people, but hey, it's Reno. He also has a good beer selection. The staff is also very knowledgeable. There is a Reserve List for higher end wines, and you can bring food from nearby restaurants to the bar.

Ole Bridge has a lot of ales and are starting to appreciate the art of the pilsner. It looks very old-fashioned with wooden walls, but is usually filled with 20-somethings and college kids. **The Jungle** (formerly a wine bar) still has a wine menu but now focuses on trendy cocktails. **West 2nd Street Bar** used to be a dive bar but with the closing of Cortez, it has cornered the karaoke market and is now filled with a much younger, more energetic crowd. **Tonic** is a small nightclub that gets DJ's late, late into the night. **Our Bar** has a pool table and darts and food. **Sierra Tap House** has a lot of Sierra Nevada beer on tap and is popular in the summer when people hang out outside. They recently expanded and now have a pool table and breathing room. **Waterfall** is a bar and hookah lounge that recently expanded. **3rd Street Bar** is for an older crowd that listens to old rock and blues. They have amateur stand up on Wednesday nights. **5 Star** is a LGBTQIA 24-hour bar that also attracts a few straight curious people and bachelorette parties. I sometimes take dates there, because A. they love to dance, and B. I don't have to worry about getting cock-blocked. **Faces** is a newly opened LGBTQIA dance club.

This is physically, the perfect nightlife district. Socially, however, as mentioned above, it is heavy on college kids, service industry 20-somethings, and a smattering of fixed income (disability, social security, pension) oldies. You also get the adventurous or in-the-know tourists.

As a tourist, you can start the night in any one of the many fine eateries in this area. Keep in mind, almost 90% of the restaurants and bars in this area were not around in 1995, in fact, I only think four were, so we're not talking about old, crusty places that have been taking advantage of tourists forever, places you'll find everywhere in most all tourist zones in all the major cities, especially on the East Coast and in Western Europe.

Also keep in mind that there is no infantile curfew in Reno. We're all adults here. We can decide when we've had enough and cut ourselves off. So typically, the college crowd drinks in their apartments, dorms, houses, etc. on the cheap before going out and start showing up at 10 PM and maxing out at 11 PM and at 2 AM disperse to all sorts of late night bars and after parties or simply go to bed.

The story is different for the 20-something service industry crowd that has loads of tips to spend and recycle to other bartenders. Restaurant bartenders and waitresses start getting off around 10 and 11 PM. So basically, the Reno party doesn't even start until 11 PM. At 1:30 AM, this gives outsiders the skewed impression that the vast majority of people in Reno are alcoholics who drink all night. At 1:30 AM, most outsiders are lit up asking for directions back to their casinos or taking the six-block Lyft ride. After 2 AM, a few bars will stay open to 3 AM depending on the crowd, but there are only three places that routinely open after 3 AM, and they are **Tonic, Rack,** and **1Up**. **Doc's** is 24 hours, but it sits precariously on the east side of Virginia St. With baseball season, they get some post-Freight House stragglers.

The Freight House "District" (Downtown Reno)

The heck if I know why they call it a district, it's a simple complex next to the baseball stadium in southeast downtown. When it first opened, it was a great party scene, but recently, it's been dying. They close it completely during the winter. They have a Mexican restaurant **Arroyo** downstairs that has a ton of tequilas. They usually have a cover charge of $5 to go upstairs to the open air deck until after the game is over. Upstairs there's

Duffy's Ale House which also serves food, **Bugsy's Sports Bar & Grill**, and **250 Lounge**. Duffy's has a good selection of beer and a middle, island bar with another small bar just outside where there's also a dance and stage area. Bugsy's doesn't have a good beer selection, but you can watch the baseball game from there, and if you're lucky, you get a table right next to the window and it's like you have some cool VIP box. 250 Lounge is a medium-sized nightclub that picks up later on. In the spring and summer, it can be a fun venue especially at the tail end of a baseball game you get a good mix of all sorts of drunk people. **Mellow Fellow** across W 2nd Street and has 40 beers on tap.

The Rest of Downtown Reno

Precariously positioned just south of the river on the west side is the newly opened **The Eddy**, a derivative container park with three shipping container bars and a big yard where you can play cornhole and other outdoor, hipster bar games. South of the river and on the east side of town is the newly opened **Bundox Bocce at Renaissance Hotel**, an indoor adult playground with seven bocce courts, skee ball, shuffle board, a restaurant, and bar.

Harrah's has **Sapphire Lounge**, but nobody goes there. Where people do go is the 1st floor in the east building, **Zone 21** where there's beer pong and blackjack dealers who look like Hooter's waitresses and I think it's every hour one of them jumps on a small stage to dance off beat and too fast. But, you know, who cares right. They also have the recently opened **Stage at the Zone** a free live music venue. There's also a dirty, dark dive bar called **Shooter's** that is not one of those hipster dive bars full of hipsters drinking PBR. This is a REAL dive bar with old dudes and young, mean-looking dudes and sassy bartender women to keep everyone in line. **Doc's** across Harrah's on W 2nd St is a cleaner, brighter bar and is open 24-hours.

Of course, there are other bars in Reno. In order of where I might go on a Thursday, Friday or Saturday night to where I would rarely go, we start with the fastest growing hipster enclave in Reno, Midtown which increasingly reminds me of Valencia and 16th in San Franny but has actually eclipsed them.

Midtown

Cal Ave (Midtown North)

Cal Ave, yes, it's called "Cal Ave" to locals, and that's a fine abbreviation, short for California Avenue, has five bars in the area and a strip club, **Wild Orchid** not to mention a mile long from first bar to the last bar on the other end. There is **Ceol** is an authentic Irish bar, but the loud Irish folk music can be a bit much. **The Loving Cup** (formerly The Biggest Little City Club, formerly Satellite and was one of the hippest new bars in Reno back in the day). **1864 Tavern** is an awesome, classic cocktail bar that uses all fresh ingredients. **St. James** has a big beer selection and a nice upstairs patio. St. James is also a popular club on Friday and Saturday nights, mostly locals. Although **Brewer's Cabinet** is not technically on Cal Ave, it's close enough and serves eclectic beer as well as eclectic, natural food. I'm also adding three bars within three blocks of Cal Ave, **Pignic Pub & Patio**, **Royce** (somewhat of a wine bar), and **Red Rock**. You can now bar crawl from downtown to Midtown without several blocks of sobriety.

Photo: Just in case you forget what city you're in. St. James Infirmary bar

Midtown *(Central)*

Unlike rowdy, crazy, tourist downtown, Midtown is a rather mellow, easy-going party district. There is **Z Bar** a formerly scary dive bar (Zephyr) turned craft cocktail bar, **Picasso & Wine** (a wine bar and painting class joint), **Silver Peak** (bar and grill with a very nice upstairs patio and a sister bar downtown), and the **Reno Public House** (a swank hipster bar with lots of beer and tiled and hard walls that make it twice as loud as it should be) with a nice outdoor patio. **Chapel** moved from Mt Rose St to the old 1099 Club location at 1099 S Virginia. It is now over twice the size with two patios and twice as many hipsters. **Brasserie St. James** is HUGE with two bars and two dining areas, a small pool/darts room, and one patio area on the first floor and then two large patio areas outside on the second floor. It is definitely a game changer and Midtown's large anchor. Midtown reminds me of Valencia & 16th in San Francisco minus Mission & 16th ghetto next block over although Reno almost mirrors the hipster-next-door-to-the-Mexican-neighborhood motif. **Death & Taxes** has great cocktails. **Shea's** is open 24 hours and has a big punk scene. Do me a favor, when you meet an older local, just say Shea's and watch their reaction. If there is none, they've never partied hard in Reno. If they smile, they've had good to borderline scary times there. If the blood drains from their face, well, that's Shea's. **Press Start** (a video arcade with a small bar) **Pinon Bottle Co** (where you can pick your beers from a cooler), and **The Saint** (a small live-music venue) are the most recent additions.

Midtown South

There is a concentration of bars and restaurants at the south end of Midtown. It is located at S Virginia St and Mt Rose St (not to be confused with Mt Rose Highway). Every now and then or on off nights, I hang out here, a two-square-block area that includes six restaurants: **Si Amigo, Miguel's, Bangkok Cuisine, Moo Dang, Sushi Pier 2**, and **Mario's**, and four bars: **40 Mile Saloon, Coach's Bar & Grill, Polo Lounge**, and **Midtown Wine Bar**. If you are inclined to walk another block or two, you can also find **The Point** lounge, **Filthy McNasty's** Irish bar, **Lulou's**, **Gas Lamp** restaurant, **Rapscallion's** seafood restaurant, and **Lucke's Saloon**.

Polo Lounge had a weird thing going. Usually a 40+ hangout including a not-too-shabby clientele, but every now and then, you get the after-hours restaurant server crowd and gold-diggers. Coach's is just a mellow, casual hangout after hours when all the other places have closed, even on Sunday nights. It cut its off-night hours to 2 AM. Midtown Wine Bar usually has live music. They often have **Tammy Tam Tam** who also sings for Flock of 80z and Steel Breeze cover bands which perform at Brew Bros and Rum Bullions.

LEX at Grand Sierra Resort (GSR)

Reno has experienced some club game-changers. Shy Clown and American Band Stand were the clubs back in the day, but the first mega-club in Reno was Reno Live where electronica was relegated to the basement. Electronic Dance Music (EDM) is now the premiere dance club music with millionaire European and Canadian DJs in Vegas. Then 210 North replaced Reno Live and blew everyone away with its amazing décor including a beautiful wall of chain curtains welcoming you as you ascended a long escalator upstairs. Well, forget all that. LEX blows them all away with a Vegas style, huge party hall and a thoughtful lounge in front to take a break from all the action. LEX is simply amazing, and with a $20 cover for locals ($30 for tourists) and $6 beers, it's an accessible club, unlike the ones in Vegas where you wait two hours in line, pay $50, and then get screwed over further with $10 beers. There's a pool in the middle that often gets visited upon by drunks. On Sundays, you can actually swim there without getting thrown out. With Rise closed, this is the apex club in Reno for the foreseeable future. Unfortunately, you must first get patted down more intimately than the TSA. Recently, attendance has been falling.

If you need a break from LEX, there's also **Boots and Daisy Dukes**, a country line dancing venue located at the William Hill Sport Book on Thursday, Friday, and Saturday nights after 10 PM. DJ Jamie G, formerly of Mustangs at the GSR, was one of Reno's gems who both spun country music and taught line dancing until he sadly passed away in 2015.

Edge at the Peppermill

This is a big, fat nightclub full of equal parts tourists and locals who love clubbing but are tired of downtown. My friends sometimes go there to celebrate parties and get a table and bottle service. The problem for me is that I don't dance unless I'm plastered, and otherwise, I'm part of the dude crust. This is like piecrust. It is a quarter or semi-circle crust of dudes around the dance floor, solo or with a friend or two, standing there with a beer bottle, watching, watching like vultures at all the hot women on the dance floor and not a single one of them will ever approach one unless she unwittingly stumbles right into the pie crust, after which they will giggle and snort to one another while one boldly starts dancing with her only to have her turn around and return to the safety of the center of the dance floor. They are like little kids too afraid to go to the deep end of the pool, clinging desperately to the sides of the pool and peeing. I used to be part of that pie crust until I finally realized just what I was a part of. It probably has other names like loser corral, nerd pen, creep herd, vulture fence, the event horizon (for super nerds), the Pathetic Rim. I just like the dude crust, it sounds gross. Also, I and my friends have been roofied there. It may not be endemic of Peppermill but just any big club, but always be careful to watch your drinks. When you've only had three drinks and want to fight everyone, sleep with everyone, or fall asleep, chances are, you've been roofied. "Roofies" are not Ropinol anymore. They're often prescription sleeping drugs like Ambien and can come in liquid form. They also give you horrendous headache and vertigo hangovers.

"College Row"

College row, the elongated row of bars along North Virginia covering a mile and including four college bars (Corkscroo, Rick's Pizza, Waldorf, and Archie's), is sad except for Thursday college nights, when every bar gets packed. **Corkscroo** on Virginia and 9th Street is a bar and grill that used to be a dive but had a nice makeover and name change. **Blind Onion** now serves pizzas inside. **Rick's Pizza** replaced the Wolf's Den which was Fritz's, the go to place for underaged kids you found out were underaged on MySpace. All four of these bars serve food. **Waldorf** is the go-to bar on Thursday nights to pick up on college coeds and drink amazingly cheap huge pitchers of beer. It's called Little Waldorf, but it is large with a front room, two pool tables, and a back room for dancing. **Archie's**, the furthest north, is open 24 hours, is two stories and has a pool table. All these places also get packed after Nevada football and basketball games. Nevada archery games, not so much. In addition to hitting on college coeds, college bars have the best drink specials in like the universe. FYI, when talking about the school, you say UNR. When talked about sports, they're called Nevada.

One of the best college football games I've ever seen in my life was the 2007 matchup between Nevada and Boise State in which they tied for the highest-scoring game in modern-day FBS history. Colin Kaepernick was the Nevada quarterback. Boise eventually won after four overtimes. I watched that game at Foley's, now **Lucky Beaver**. One of the biggest chokes in college football history was the 2010 matchup between Nevada and Boise State in which the Boise State kicker missed an easy 26-yard field goal with two seconds left that could have given Boise State the win but left them tied. Then in overtime he missed a 29-yard field goal, and Nevada made a field goal to upset the then 3rd ranked Boise State which could have gone all the way to the national championship bowl game. I watched the ending of that game at Imperial. Some of my friends had attended the game in Reno but left early because it was too cold. They only missed the greatest victory in Nevada history.

East Fourth Street

East Fourth Street covers the old Highway 40 that went from Reno to San Francisco before they built Interstate 80. The old Highway 40 was lined with what was then, brand new motels catering to the new American car lifestyle. Oh, weren't those the days? The motels today have turned into some of the nastiest roach motels you've ever seen filled with druggies, ex-cons, sex offenders, criminals-on-the-run, countless people who have lost their homes to gambling or alcoholism, prostitutes, divorcees, and low-income newcomers (myself included at one point). Needless to say, E 4th Street has a seedy reputation that is only enhanced by two strip clubs. To make things even worse, the business association in the area, E4 has embraced the moniker, "The Red Light District."

With that said, the bars there are not as bad as one might think, and are actually quite charming and safe. The bartenders there have a living to make, and I am sure they have a no-nonsense attitude toward assholes who don't pay for drinks scaring away decent regulars who do pay for drinks. None-the-less, I have yet to see many hot, young people except the closer you get to downtown as in the **Lincoln Lounge** and **Louis' Basque Corner** 2nd floor bar which unfortunately does not open late and is way too bright.

The BlueBird Nightclub (formerly PB&J, formerly Bodegas Nightclub, formerly the Underground) is a concert venue and sometimes has cool burner parties. Speaking of Burners, there is a real Burner hotel called the **Morris Hotel** with uniquely décored rooms and a small bar and lounge, although code and construction is putting their existence in question. **Abby's Highway 40** is a fun hole-in-the-wall with an owner and bartender, **Donny Schwarz** who knows a lot about old school Reno and has been a bartender here for 39 years. Supposedly, he's worked at over 70 bars in Reno. **Studio on 4th** next door is a nice cabaret. **The Depot Craft Brewery Distillery** recently opened. **Pigeon Head Brewery** also recently opened and is located on 5th Street. Overnight the area has become a brewery district which is fitting, because in the old days there were brewers and bottling companies on E 4th Street. The **Spice House** strip club is actually part of the old Rainier Brewing Company Bottling Plant. Spokane Street is not named after the city of Spokane but actually Spokane Street in Seattle near Rainier headquarters.

South Reno

South Reno, before you get to the McCarran Loop that rings Reno and Sparks, has over a dozen bars all dotting on or near Virginia Street but not close enough to do a bar crawl. I used to be a regular at Foley's because the owner was like Benny Hill and liked to surround himself with hot, busty waitresses and bartenders. There was one point around 2007 and 2008 when there were more hot workers at Foley's than hot women just hanging out at any bar or club in Reno. **Lucky Beaver** from Stateline took over Foley's spot. **Jox** is 24 hours and rumor has it, strippers go there late at night. But then I guess, strippers go to any 24-hour bar after getting off work at 3 AM. A hidden gem is **Hellfire Saloon** in the Mira

Loma shopping center (formerly located on S Virginia St near South Meadows).

The Great Northwest Bar & Grill District

In 1995 there were two apartment complexes and two bars: Summit Saloon and Bully's. Now there are ten bars and approximately 17 million apartment complexes. So who lives in new apartment complexes you say? Hmmm. Single people and college kids. The Great Northwest had its day, but as apartment prices are going down, more and more families are moving in. None-the-less, with eight bar-and-grills, most sports oriented, it is the "Great Northwest Bar & Grill District." Plenty of married people, families, middle-aged dudes getting away from their wives, etc. but not so many young'uns except the local college students. Back in the day, **Bully's** at 2005 Sierra Highlands used to be a big college hangout. It may still get big college crowds every now and then, but I haven't checked lately. Closer to UNR at King's Row and McCarran you get this little patch of action including **Chewy'n'Jug's**, **Beck's Brew House**, and **Blind Onion** pizzeria.

Far South Reno

There's the Far South past the McCarran Loop, but this is another bar and grill district for families and middle-aged dudes escaping their wives and also a few rich older folk. It is way too far even for a Lyft. I always thought **Sierra Gold** was a casino, but it is a surprisingly nice, large bar with three pool tables. I like going to **Flowing Tide 2** every now and then to sing karaoke on Friday nights. It's a bar-and-grill with a nautical theme. There are three Flowing Tides in Reno. **Whispering Vine** is cougarville and has a bar but closes at 9 PM.

Sparks

Sparks had a small nightlife district on Victorian Ave on Thursday nights coinciding with Thursday Night Farmers' Markets, but it became too much of a party scene with fights and at one point a shooting. The City of Sparks decided to kill the event by moving it into a parking lot further west.

On top of that, the police also have nothing to do out there except give out DUIs and traffic tickets. Sparks does not want a nightlife scene, and it will not get one. I only can remember wistfully the great days of the Thursday Night Market at **O'Ski's**, **Great Basin**, **Paddy'n'Irene's**,

Victorian Saloon, Mummer's (formerly Alley, formerly Vixen), **Cantina Los Tres Hombres** Mexican restaurant and live band venue, and even Trader Dick's inside the Nugget Casino, closed and infamous for the sight of an ugly fist, knife, and gun fight between Hell's Angels and Vagos.

Sparks also has bar-and-grills all over the place catering to locals. There's also plenty of little quaint dive bars in Sparks inside the McCarran Loop.

North Valleys

Stead has three bars, and nobody goes there except locals, because it's a long Lyft ride, and the same goes for Lemmon Valley and Sun Valley, not to mention the fact that these are rural bars and tend to have an older crowd. If that's your cup of tea, I don't judge.

Okay So Where Do Middle-Aged Folk Hang Out?

A lot of middle-aged people don't hang out, at least not in Reno. Most of them are home by midnight. They do the restaurant, concert, theatre thing. Many also simply do happy hour or hang out at wine bars in wine stores. However, there is a growing middle-aged nightlife in Reno. Go to **Roxy's** at Eldorado, **Polo Lounge, Napa Sonoma** restaurant, **Hellfire Saloon, The Point, Midtown Wine, Whispering Vine, Whole Foods, The Grill at Quail Corners, West Street Wine, 3rd Street Bar,** or hang out at the bar of any upscale restaurant or wine store. If you're more into the blue collar scene, hang out at any sports bar-and-grill. If you're poor, hang out at any dive bar.

Bar Rescue

Opening your own bar can be kindly viewed as a gracious act of charity for people who like to work evenings and nights, perhaps artists who audition during the day, college kids, thieves, and an odd coterie of anti-establishment folks who hate day jobs. It has one of the highest rates of failure and very low profits with incessant, ubiquitous product shrinkage and unregistered sales. A TV show called Bar Rescue highlights this fact and tries to rescue failing bars with a snazzy makeover. The formula is pretty played out: clean it up, fresh coat of paint, new furniture, make it look cosmopolitan, give it a kitschy locally typecast theme, and replace every drink with corporate label cocktails that sponsor the show. Two bars here have undergone a Bar Rescue, **Oak Tavern** in Sparks and Money Bar in Reno which reverted back to Murphy's Law before being bought and changed to **Jimmy B's.**

Digression on "Hipster" Bartenders and Waiters

Before big chains and corporations, people traveling the country would always be fearful of not being welcome at a local establishment. Even worse, if you were a minority, you could be swiftly exited out the front door. Or worse, you just got bad service and some bigot might put too much salt in your food, overcook it, or deposit any type of bodily fluid into it. Not only were people horrified of bad food, an expensive waste back then, but they were horrified of bad service. The regional and then national chains addressed that by standardizing service levels and ironically, over the years, demanding better and better "world-class" customer service in exchange for fewer benefits, less training, less supervision, less authority, and lower pay. Hmmm. In any event, young people eagerly staffed the major chains and corporate restaurants and gave the performance of a lifetime with ubiquitous smiles and imperturbable charm.

Some hipsters find this not only annoying but symbolic of the fakery of chains and corporate service. Instead of simply toning the charm down and offering genuine, customized customer service, empowering and involving their front line workers, they simply don't push the whole customer service thing on their staff. You can't blame many servers to interpret this as, act apathetic and be apathetic about customer service. So go ahead and text, take long breaks, socialize with friends in front of waiting customers, and generally treat customers like bothersome losers who have to earn your respect by becoming regulars and tipping them outrageously. Otherwise, fuck off.

I am also so fricking sick and tired of "barista-bartenders" who think they're working at Starbucks and all they need to do is make your drinks, expect a $1 tip, and walk off to update their Facebook and socialize with friends at the end of the bar. I'm not asking them to be my best friend or therapist, but would it kill you to check on me once an hour especially if the place is slow and nearly empty. People do not go to bars to drink alcohol and watch TV. They can do that at home. This is not your fricking living room, it's a place of business, and your boss's mortgage is on the line. Take some damn pride in your work and value your customers. If you're a bar owner, do yourself a favor and get friends to be secret shoppers to see if your bartenders are assholes.

What Are the Best Bars in Reno?

Every year the local rag, Reno Gazette-Journal (RGJ), and the weekly indie-rag, Reno News & Review (RN&R), come out with their "Best in Reno" or "Best of Reno" or whatever. In 2012, as I mentioned before, readers voted Naan'n'Kabob the 2nd best Indian restaurant in Reno proving that most readers know nothing. Here is my list:

Best Dance Club

1. The Rack (Fri, Sat) 2. Brew Bros (Thu, Fri, Sat) 3. Edge (Fri, Sat)

Best Meat Market

1. The Rack (Fri, Sat) 2. Brew Bros (Thu, Fri, Sat) 3. Imperial (Wed)

Best Coed Bar

1. Waldorf (Thu) 2. Imperial (Wed) 3. Pub & Sub

Best Cougar Bar

1. Midtown Wine 2. Polo Lounge 3. Napa-Sonoma

Best Karaoke

1. W 2nd St Bar (7-nights-a-week) 2. The Point (Fri, Sat) 3. CalNeva (Fri, Sat)

Best Cocktail Bar

1. Chapel 2. Death & Taxes 3. The Jungle

Best Whiskey List

1. Chapel 2. Death & Taxes 3. Hard Water House

Best Bar for Pool and Hanging Out

1. Imperial 2. Waterfall 3. Little Waldorf

Best Chain Sports Bars

1. Bully's 2. Sparky's 3. Buffalo Wild Wings

Best Obscure Bar

1. Jub Jub's Thirst Parlor 2. Hideout 3. Man Cave

Best Hipster Bar

1. Reno Public House 2. Chapel 3. Blind Dog Tavern

Best Reno Non-Hipster, Non-Ironic Dive Bar

1. Shooter's 2. Davidson's 3. Doc's

Best Sparks Non-Hipster, Non-Ironic Dive Bar

1. Copenhagen 2. Outer Limits 3. Mecca Lounge

Strangest Bar

1. DILLIGAS 2. Air Base Inn 3. Blender Bar at Silver Legacy

Most Obscure Unknown Non-Hipster Midtownish Bar

1. Alibi 2. Hub 3. Tiger Tom's

Best Bar If It Were Closer to Town

1. Buckhorn's 2. Sierra Gold 3. Buffalo Wild Wings

Best Late Night Club

1. 1Up 2. Tonic 3. The Rack

Best Micro-Brewery

1. Pigeon Head Brewery 2. Great Basin 2. Silver Peak

Worst Bar Name

1. Filthy McNasty's 2. Our Bar 3. 1Up

All the Bars in Reno, Sparks, and Sun Valley

When I say "dive bar" I don't mean that as a pejorative. The décor is old and worn out, it may be full of old barflies, but it could be fun and have a few young'uns. When I say "hipster bar" all I'm saying is that the people there have hipster fashion not necessarily a hipster lifestyle.

Also, keep in mind that bars are constantly opening and closing. I highlight new bars and cross out old bars in the last couple years, because I feel this helps people keep track of what has closed or opened recently.

Reno
North Valleys
Stead

- Sneaker's Bar & Grill   bar & grill   13870 Stead Bl at Lear
- Hangar Bar   bar   10603 Stead Bl at Silver Lake
- Air Base Inn   dive bar   9750 N Virginia St

Lemmon Valley

- Mudslingers ~~Spurs Saloon~~   bar   9275 Lemmon Dr north of Surge
- The Wayside   bar   9015 Lemmon Dr north of Surge
- The Bar   bar   Lemmon Dr at Limber Pine Dr

North Reno

- Man Cave   bar   4600 N Virginia St behind the gas station!
- Woodrow's Tap Room   dive bar   4755 N Virginia St
- Mixers   bar   2900 Clear Acre Ln

Northwest Reno

- Bully's Sports Bar & Grill   bar & grill   2005 Sierra Highlands
- Bully's Sports Bar & Grill   bar & grill   1640 Robb Dr at Mae Anne
- Pierce's Pub   bar & grill   6148 Mae Anne at Robb Dr
- Moxie's Spirits & Dining   bar w rest.   6275 Sharlands Ave west of Robb
- Flowing Tide Pub   bar & grill   10580 N McCarran Bl at W 7th St
- Whispering Vine   wine bar   4201 W 4th St
- Flowing Tide   bar & grill   9570 S McCarran Bl at W 4th St
- Pinot's Palette   wine & paint bar   5110 Mae Anne Ave #702
- Beck's Brew House   bar   3611 Kings Row north at McCarran Bl

- Chewy'n'Jugs   bar & grill   3629 Kings Row

University

- Archie's   bar & grill   2195 N Virginia St
- The Little Waldorf Saloon   bar & grill   1661 N Virginia St
- Rick's Pizza ~~Wolf's Den~~   bar & pizza   1305 N Virginia St
- Corkscroo   bar & grill   10 E 9th St at N Virginia St
- Pub & Sub   bar & grill   1000 Ralston St at W 10th St

Downtown

Casinos

Silver Legacy   *407 N Virginia St*
- Aura   nightclub   1st floor west
- Silver Baron Lounge   lounge   1st floor
- Rum Bullions   nightclub   2nd floor north
- Blender Bar   WTF?   2nd floor north
- Drinx   lounge   2nd floor west

Eldorado   *345 N Virginia St*
- Stadium Bar   sports bar   1st floor west
- Brew Bros   bar & rest.   2nd floor north
- Roxy's   lounge   2nd floor north
- Cin Cin Bar & Lounge   lounge   2nd floor south
- NoVi   country   2nd floor south

Circus Circus   *500 N Sierra St*
- El Jefe   club & rest.   2nd floor south

Harrah's   *219 N Center St*
- Sapphire Lounge   nightclub   1st floor, west building
- The Stage @ The Zone   nightclub   1st floor, east building

Freight House   250 Evans Ave

- Duffy's Ale House   bar & grill   2nd floor north
- Bugsy's Sports Bar   bar & grill   2nd floor southeast
- 250 Lounge   nightclub   2nd floor west

Downtown Other

- Mellow Fellow   bar & grill   300 E 2nd St across baseball stadium
- Doc Holiday's   24-hour bar   120 E 2nd St btwn Center and Lake St's
- Men's Club   strip club   270 N Lake St at Commercial Row
- Shooter's   dive bar   434 N Virginia St btwn 4th and 5th St's
- ~~Stamp Social Club~~   ~~bar~~   ~~50 S Virginia St (closes at 11 PM)~~

- The Eddy   container park   16 S Sierra St (closes at 11:30 PM)
- Foxy Olive   small bar   220 Mill St at Lake St
- Bundox Bocce   bar & games   1 Lake St (inside Renaissance Hotel)
- Swiss Chalet   dive bar   501 Mill St at High St
- Mill Street Still & Brew   brewpub   490 Mill St
- Red Rock   hipster bar   241 S Sierra St north of Liberty
- Royce   wine bar   115 Ridge St
- Pignic Pub & Patio   bar & grill   235 Flint St

West Street Area

- 3rd St Blues   live band bar   125 W 3rd St btwn West and Sierra St's
- 1Up   hipster nightclub   214 W Commercial Row at West St
- Tonic   nightclub   231 W 2nd St
- Faces ~~The Trocadero Bar~~   LGBQTIA club   239 W 2nd St
- Headquarters ~~Singer Social Club~~   bar   219 W 2nd St
- Imperial Bar & Lounge bar & grill   150 N Arlington Ave at W 2nd St
- Blind Dog Tavern ~~Monolith Bar~~   hipster bar   100 N Arlington
- Sierra Tap House   bar   253 W 1st St (by the river)
- The Jungle   bar   246 W 1st St
- Our Bar   bar   211 W 1st St
- Five Star Saloon   LGBQTIA club   132 West St
- Crafted Palette   wine & paint bar   130 West St
- ~~Rock Bar~~   ~~concert hall~~   ~~211 N Virginia St at W 2nd St~~
- ~~Se7en~~   ~~bar~~   ~~148 West St, behind West Street Wine Bar~~
- West St Wine Bar   wine bar   148 West St
- Waterfall   bar & hookah   134 W 2nd St
- Silver Peak Grill   brewery & grill   135 N Sierra St at W 1st St
- Ole Bridge Pub   bar   50 N Sierra St , overlooking Truckee River
- The Stick   sports bar   95 N Sierra St #101
- Cargo (at Whitney Peak)   concert   255 N Virginia St
- Liberty Food & Wine Exchange ~~Reno Provisions~~   bar & market   100 N Sierra St
- The Rack   bowling alley & bar   101 N Virginia St

West Reno

- ~~Val's Midtown Lounge~~   ~~dive bar~~   ~~611 W 2nd St at Bell St~~
- Brickie's Tavern   bar & grill   706 W 2nd St at Washington St
- Patio   LGBQTIA   600 W 5th St at Bell St
- Momma Bears Lounge   dive bar   211 Keystone Ave at W 2nd St
- Knucklehead's Bar & Grill   dive bar & grill, live band   405 Vine St at W 4th St
- Pizza Baron   bar & pizza   1155 W 4th St
- Big Horn Bar & Grill   bar & grill   1325 W 7th St
- Gateway Inn Lounge   dive bar   1275 Stardust St

East 4th Street

- Louis' Basque Corner Bar   bar   301 E 4th St 2nd Floor
- Davidson's Distillery   live band biker bar   275 E 4th St
- Lincoln Lounge   hipster bar & patio   306 E 4th St
- Record Street Brewing Co.   brewery   324 E 4th St
- The Depot Craft Brewery Distillery   brewery, distillery, rest. 325 E 4th St
- Lead Dog Brewing Co.   brewery   415 E 4th St
- Abby's Highway 40   dive bar   424 E 4th St
- Studio on 4th   bar & cabaret   432 E 4th St
- BlueBird Nightclub ~~PB&J~~   nightclub   555 E 4th St
- Under the Rose   brewery   559 E 4th St
- Pigeon Head Brewery   brewery   840 E 5th St
- Spice House   dive strip club   310 Spokane St at E 4th St
- Alturas Bar   dive bar   1044 E 4th St
- Fantasy Girls   strip club   1095 E 4th St
- The Cadillac Lounge   LGBQTIA   1114 E 4th St
- DILLIGAS Saloon   swinger's club   1303 E 4th St

East Reno

- IMBIB Custom Brews   microbrewery   785 E 2nd St
- Sneaker's   billiards   1100 E Plumb
- Vassar Lounge   dive bar   1545 Vassar St east of Kietzke (behind Long John's Silver)
- Player's Club   bar & grill   2590 E 2nd St (just north of Grand Sierra)
- The Key Club   strip club   1060 Telegraph St south of Mill St
- Floyd's Fireside Chat   dive bar   698 Kietzke Ln south of Mill St
- Joe Bob's Bar & Grill   bar & grill   4840 Mill St

Grand Sierra Resort   2500 E 2nd St

- LEX   nightclub   main floor north
- Boots and Daisy Dukes at William Hill Sports Book   country nightclub   main floor middle
- Butterfly Bar and Cascade Lounge ~~WET~~   bar and lounge main floor middle
- The Reserve   wine bar   main floor middle

Midtown

Cal Ave

- Upscale Lounge at Creazian   club (Sat only)   425 S Virginia St

- Ceol Irish Pub — Irish bar — 538 S Virginia St
- SixFour Growlers — beer shop — 555 S Virginia St #105
- Wild Orchid Gentlemen's Club — strip club — 515 S Virginia St
- Loving Cup — hipster bar — 188 Cal Ave at Plumas
- St James Infirmary — bar & patio — 445 Cal Ave, east of Arlington Ave
- Brewer's Cabinet — hipster bar/rest. — 475 S Arlington Ave
- 1864 Tavern — cocktail bar — 290 Cal Ave

Midtown

- Jub Jub — live band bar — 71 S Wells Ave, south of E 2nd St
- Hideout — dive bar — 240 S Park St south of Mill St
- Shea's Tavern — dive bar — 715 S Virginia St, at St Lawrence St
- Mountain Music Parlor — recital hall — 735 S Center St
- Pinon Bottle Co — bar — 777 S Center St
- The Saint — live band venue — 755 S Virginia St
- The Glass Die — board game parlour — 675 Holcomb Ave
- Picasso & Wine — wine & paint bar — 148 Vassar St
- Reno Public House — hipster bar — 33 St Lawrence St
- Brasserie St. James — brewery/grill — 901 S Center St
- Chapel — hipster bar — 1099 S Virginia St at Vassar
- Death & Taxes — cocktail bar — 30 Cheney St just east of Virginia
- Z Bar — cocktail bar — 1074 S Virginia St at Vassar
- Silver Peak (Midtown) — brewery & grill, patio — 124 Wonder St at Holcomb

Midtown South

- McNasty's — bar — 1718 Holcomb Ave at Regency
- Alibi Lounge — 24-hr dive bar — 125 Casazza Dr east of Wells Ave
- Press Start — bar & arcade — 1413 S Virginia St
- 40 Mile Saloon — hipster bar — 1495 S Virginia St, at Mt Rose St
- ~~Men Wielding Fire — bar & BBQ — 1537 S Virginia St~~
- Midtown Wine Bar — wine bar — 1527 S Virginia St
- Polo Lounge — bar & nightclub — 1559 S Virginia St
- Coach's — bar & grill — 1573 S Virginia St
- The Point — lounge/karaoke — 1601 S Virginia St
- Shenanigan's Old English Pub — bar & grill — 77 W Plumb Ln

Wells Ave

- Ryan's Saloon — live band dive bar — 924 S Wells Ave at Taylor
- Wonder Bar — dive bar — 1195 S Wells Ave at Wonder
- Lucke's Saloon — dive bar — 1455 S Wells Ave south of Broadway
- ~~Corrigan's Bit O'Ireland — dive bar — 1526 S Wells Ave~~

South Reno

- Joe Bob's Chicken Wings   bar & grill   7689 S Virginia St (at Huffaker)
- Bronco Billy's Saloon   dive bar   145 Hillcrest Dr west of Virginia St
- Clary's Bar & Grill   bar & grill   2780 S Virginia St (across Peppermill)
- Hub   dive bar   3098 Kietzke Ln, at Gentry
- Tiger Tom's   dive bar   196 Gentry Way, east of Virginia St
- Knockouts Sports Bar   bar & grill   551 E Moana Ln
- Master's   dive bar   923 W Moana Ln, east of Lakeside
- Swill Coffee & Wine   coffee & wine bar   3366 Lakeside Ct
- Q's Billiard Club   billiards   3350 S Virginia St north of Moana
- ~~Reno Pub and Games~~   ~~bar & video games~~   ~~3340 Kietzke Ln~~
- Carl's Pub   LGBQTIA   3310 S Virginia St north of Moana
- Lucky Beaver   bar & grill   3655 S Virginia St
- Jimmy B's ~~Murphy's Law~~   bar & grill   180 W Peckham Ln #1070
- We Olive & Wine Bar of Reno   wine bar   4991 S Virginia St
- Great Basin   brewery & grill   5525 S Virginia St at McCarran Bl
- Whole Foods Bar   bar & grill   6139 S Virginia St at Neil Rd
- Legend's Grill   bar & grill   6015 S Virginia St
- Coach's #2   bar & grill   4050 S McCarran Bl

Peppermill   2707 S Virginia St

- Edge   nightclub   second floor (right from escalators)
- Terrace Lounge   lounge   second floor (left from escalators)
- Fireside Lounge   lounge   main floor
- Pub   regular bar   main floor

Far South Reno

- Hard Water House ~~Joe Bob's~~   bar & rest.   7689 S Virginia St
- Flowing Tide 3   bar & grill   4690 Longley Ln at Mira Loma
- Sneaker's Bar & Grill   bar & grill   3923 S McCarran Bl
- Sierra Gold   bar & grill   680 South Meadows Pkwy
- ~~Hellfire~~   ~~live band bar~~   ~~9825 S Virginia St~~
- Lounge   bar   770 South Meadows Pkwy, Suite 110
- Flowing Tide 2   bar & grill   465 South Meadows Pkwy
- Beer NV   taproom   15 Foothill Rd #1
- BJ's Brewery   brewery & rest. 13999 S Virginia St (at Summit Mall)
- ~~Buffalo Wild Wings~~   ~~bar & grill~~   ~~13967 S Virginia St #914~~
- Smokin Bully's   regular bar   18150 Wedge Pkwy, at Mt Rose Hwy
- Bully's Sports Bar & Grill   bar & grill   18156 Wedge Pkwy, at Mt Rose Hwy
- Ole Tyme Saloon   dive bar   1505 Geiger Grade Rd

Sparks

Victorian Ave

- Farah & Sons Bar ~~Burg's~~   bar   1446 Victorian Ave
- ~~Gilley's at Sparks Nugget~~   ~~country nightclub, 1100 Nugget Ave~~
- Victorian Saloon   dive bar   908 Victorian Ave
- Paddy'n'Irene's   dive bar   906 Victorian Ave
- Mummer's   live band dive bar   906 Victorian Ave
- Great Basin Brewing   brewery & grill   846 Victorian Ave
- O'Ski's   bar & grill   840 Victorian Ave

Old Sparks

- Millenium Night Club   nightclub   2100 Victorian Ave
- La Morena Bar   Mexican karaoke   2140 Victorian Ave
- Blitz Bar & Grill   bar & grill   400 S Rock Bl, south of I-80
- Bob and Lucy's Tavern   bar   1515 Oddie Bl
- Sparks Station Bar & Grill   bar & grill   1221 Commerce St at Rock Bl
- Morelli's G St Saloon   dive bar   2285 G St at El Rancho
- Mecca Lounge   dive bar   880 Holman Way at Pyramid Way
- Grumpy's Sports Bar & Grill   bar & grill   2240 Oddie Bl
- Elbow Room   dive bar   2002 Victorian Ave
- Aguita's Bar & Grill   Mexican bar & grill, nightclub   1825 Prater Way
- Bottoms Up   dive bar   1923 Prater Way
- Copenhagen Bar   dive bar   2140 Prater Way
- Coney Island   bar & grill   2644 Prater Way
- Bully's Sports Bar & Grill   bar & grill   2955 N McCarran Bl at Pyramid Way

East Sparks

- O'Cleary's Irish Pub   bar & grill   Legends
- ~~CBQ Cowboy Bar & 'Cue~~   ~~country bar~~   ~~Legends~~
- BJ's Brewery   brewery & rest.   425 Sparks Bl
- Buffalo Wild Wings   bar & grill   1560 E Lincoln Way
- Atomic Bootlegger Lounge   bar   200 N McCarran Bl (inside Sierra Sid's Casino)
- Outer Limits   dive bar   404 N McCarran Bl
- Flowing Tide   bar & grill   1450 E Prater Way at Sparks Bl
- Spiro's Sports Bar & Grill   bar & grill   1475 E Prater Way west of Sparks Bl
- Sparks Lounge   live band bar   1237 Baring Bl
- Luckie's Sports Bar   bar   608 E Prater Way at McCarran Bl
- Smokin Bully's   bar   2828 Vista Bl south of Baring
- Bully's Sports Bar & Grill   bar & grill   2898 Vista Bl south of Baring

South Sparks

- High Sierra Brewing Co.   microbrewery   865 S Rock Bl (Baldini's Casino)
- Woody's Grille & Spirits   bar & grill   960 S McCarran Bl north of Greg

Far North Sparks

- Sneaker's   bar & grill   1380 Disc Dr at Vista
- Oak Tavern   bar & grill   5215 Vista Bl at Los Altos

Spanish Springs

- Lake Bar & Grill   bar & grill   9716 Pyramid Way
- Buckhorns   regular bar   9724 Pyramid Way
- Bully's   bar & grill   9725 Pyramid Way

Sun Valley

- JR's   dive bar   5400 Sun Valley Bl at 4th Ave
- Silver Moon   dive bar   5465 Sun Valley Bl at 5th Ave
- Kelly's Bar ~~Harvey's Sun Valley Bar~~   dive bar   5544 Sun Valley Bl

Cocktails, Tropical Drinks, Wine, and Beer in Reno

If you haven't noticed, classic craft cocktails are all the rage, and I'm not talking about Screwdrivers or Slippery Nipples. I'm talking about pre-Prohibition as well as the 50's cocktail revolution made popular in the HBO show *Mad Men*. I believe Bourbon & Branch in San Francisco was the first classic cocktail bar in the region celebrating the speakeasy era. While Reno is often behind the curve on trends, Chapel (when it was at Mt Rose St) opened in 2007, was the first Reno bar to celebrate classic cocktails with bartenders in vests and ties. Unfortunately, PBR and Olympia were their bestselling drinks. Reno is now experiencing a small classic cocktail revival. Interesting to note, the corporate cesspit of Vegas didn't pick up on the classic cocktail scene until AFTER Reno.

Some background on cocktails: punch was the prototype cocktail and the word actually comes from the Hindustani word 'panch' which means five representing the five essential ingredients of arrack alcohol, sugar, lemons, water/tea, and spice. The cocktail was born in America and it is commonly accepted that 1806 is the birth date, the first time 'cocktail' was printed in a newspaper. In response to a reader's inquiry, the editor defines cocktail as a liquor composed of spirits, sugar, water, and bitters. The true test of a cocktail is the balance between all its ingredients so that it does not come across as too bitter, sweet, tart, or even "alcoholy." Americans later added egg whites to give it a creamy smooth texture. Due to the liability of salmonella poisoning, most bars avoid egg whites. There are countless cocktails now including cobblers, Collins, coolers, fizzes, flips, highballs, mulled drinks, punches, rickeys, sangaries, shrubs, slings, smashes, sours, swizzles, and toddies. The most common bitter is Angostura created by a German doctor as a medical tonic made of alcohol, herbs, and spices.

Chapel, Z Bar, 1864 Tavern, Death & Taxes, Pignic Pub & Patio, the Jungle, and **Reno Public House** are the best cocktail bars in Reno. Roxy has 50 martinis on their menu but it's basically all types of cocktails served in a martini glass. They have an Old Fashioned they call the Kentucky Martini.

Whiskey is one of the fastest growing spirits. If it's made in Scotland and Canada it is spelled "whisky" and in America and Ireland it is spelled "whiskey." Much like the wine and beer market and basically most things out there, you have a few corporations with a disproportionate chunk of the whiskey market buying up small labels and keeping the labels but watering down the product. I avoid Brown-Forman Corp. (NYSE) products like Woodford Reserve and Jack Daniel's. I avoid Diageo (LSE, NYSE) products like Bulleit, Johnnie Walker, Bushmills, Crown Royal,

Seagram's, and George Dickel. Diageo has a brilliant marketing scheme called the Orphan Barrel Project capitalizing on the huge success of long-aged **Pappy Van Winkle**. They have 20 to 26-year-old bourbon they sell for $75 to $150 a bottle. It is believe *The Internship* movie about middle-aged Google interns popularized Pappy Van Winkle 23-year-old bourbon. Death & Taxes charges $150 for a single shot of that bourbon. I tried it at Z Bar for substantially less and wasn't impressed. It goes for around $2000 a bottle online.

I used to avoid Beam, Inc., products like Jim Beam, Maker's Mark, Knob Creek, Basil Hayden's, Booker's, and Canadian Club Whisky. They planned to water down Maker's Mark from 90 to 84 proof until public outrage stopped them. But they were recently acquired by Suntory which makes Yamazaki Single Malt Sherry Cask 2013, ranked as the best whisky in the world by renowned whisky expert Jim Murray. Incidentally, three American bourbons took 2nd, 3rd, and 4th place, **William Larue (W.L.) Weller** (Sazerac Co.), **Sazerac** Rye 18 Year Old (Sazerac Co.), and **Four Roses** (Kirin Brewery Co.). In probably one of the funniest product placements in history, Bill Murray in *Lost in Translation* does a Japanese TV ad, "For relaxing times, make it Suntory time." Suntory also makes Hakushu and Hibiki whisky. Yamazaki tastes more like scotch without the overwhelming peaty flavor. You can find it at Brasserie St. James and Chapel.

I prefer Sazerac Co. (US privately owned) products like **Blanton's, Buffalo Trace, Eagle Rare, Van Winkle, Sazerac**, and **Barton**. They also make **Elmer T Lee** and **EH Taylor** if you can find and afford them. I prefer Heaven Hill Distilleries, Inc. (US privately owned) products like **Elijah Craig** and **Evan Williams**. **Hudson Bourbon** is US privately owned. Lawrenceburg Distillers Indiana (LDI) is a shady company that makes Templeton and then makes Bulleit for Diageo but doesn't want anyone to know that.

Tropical drinks are also starting to become popular again. Most Mexican restaurants will have decent margaritas. **Arroyo** at Freight House and **Cantina** at GSR probably have the largest selection of tequilas. **Rum Bullions** (Rumbullion was the original name for rum and comes from the old English slang for a brawl) has good tropical rum drinks, but it's a bit kitschy. You have to go to Smuggler's Cove in San Francisco to get real authentic tropical drinks.

Wine has also been making a comeback over the last two decades, and I'm not talking about Rombauer and Mondavi. While I always enjoy a nice, fat, thick, warm buttery chard, there are countless wine varietals missing from most restaurant and wine bar menus. **Www.winefolly.com** is a great way to introduce yourself to the new wine age and was created by a former Reno native and West St Wine Bar sommelier Madeline Puckette. A Michigan State University study found that twelve companies made up 64.4% of the US wine market in 2011 and three that made up 51.5%. E&J Gallo Winery which makes Carlo Rossi, Barefoot, Andre, Turning Leaf and Ecco Domani made up 22.8%. The Wine Group which makes Franzia, Inglenook, and Foxhorn made up 15.9%. Constellation Brands which makes Woodbridge, Arbor Mist, Clos du Bois, Robert Mondavi, Cook's and Estancia Estates made up 12.8%. Diageo (LSE, NYSE) owns Beaulieu, Sterling, Acacia, Chalone, and BV Coastal.

West St Wine Bar does an excellent job introducing you to the less known, high quality wines of the world. They now have a reserve list with pours by the ounce, a great way of getting a little taste of heaven. The one hang-up I have in Reno is why it has so many California Pinot Noirs and ignores Willamette Valley Pinot Noirs. Only **Lulou's** has a decent Willamette Valley Pinot Noir selection and that's because one of the owners is from Oregon. For whatever reason, Vegas has a lot of Willamette Valley Pinot Noirs. Unfortunately, when I last visited Willamette Valley I was displeased at how much they were copying California's fruity Pinot Noir style, although that may also be the result of global climate change. One small benefit of climate change is higher alcohol in wine. **Midtown Wine Bar** also does a good job providing an eclectic array of wines. People may not like the high wine by the glass price, but consider this: a 750mL bottle of wine retailing at $25 (like Beringer Cab Napa) pours five 5-ounce portions ($5 retail/glass). A 750mL bottle of bourbon at $25 (like Maker's Mark) pours seventeen 1.5-ounce portions ($1.50 retail/glass). Marking up the wine thrice on retail gives you $15/glass, but mark up the bourbon thrice on retail gives you $4.50/glass.

Craft/micro-brewed beer has also been making a comeback the last two decades, although I'm not a big fan of the whole IPA and Belgian beer hipster thing. Like cocktails, a beer should be balanced, and the only ingredients in real beer are water, yeast, hops, and barley malt. Just as a cocktail balances bitters and sweets, a beer should balance the bitterness of hops with the sweetness of barley malt. An IPA is overly hopped while a Belgian ale's hops make it unbearable floral or fruity. In my opinion, the ESB (Extra Special Bitter) is probably one of the most balanced beer styles, but unfortunately people think it is extra bitter. A bitter is simply an English term for pale ale. There is a great documentary called *Beer Wars* which explains how the beer oligopolies Anheuser-Busch InBev and MillerCoors have bought out independent beer companies and created a distributorship cartel.

Here's a list of what I think are great regional beers: **Battle Born Beer** (Reno, NV), **Great Basin Beer** (Sparks, NV), **Trumer** (Berkeley CA), **Gordon Biersch** (San Jose CA), **Anchor** (San Francisco CA), **Sierra Nevada** (Chico CA), **Sudwerk** (Davis CA), **Rogue** (Oregon), **Bridgeport** (Oregon), and **Deschutes** (Oregon).

Here's a list of beers that are owned by corporate conglomerates:

Anheuser-Busch Inbev owns American beers: Bud, Michelob, Natural, Busch, Rolling Rock, Ziegenbock, and foreign beers: Becks, Czechvar, Leffe, Tiger, Stella Artois, Shock Top, Bass, Hoegaarden, Boddington's, Kirin Ichiban, and Lowenbrau. They also own Monster and 180 energy drinks.

MillerCoors owns: Coors, Miller, Keystone, Icehouse, Milwaukee's Best, Olde English 800, Steel Reserve, Mickey's, Red Dog, Hamms, Leinenkugel, Henry Weinhard, Sparks and foreign beers: Blue Moon, Foster's, George Killians, Molson, Pilsner Urquell, Peroni, Grolsch, and most unbelievably, Tyskie and Caffrey's Irish Ale. Coors made Batch 19 and Third Shift Amber Lager which they tried to pawn off as hipster craft beers.

MillerCoors bought StarBev in April 2012 which includes Staropramen and other Central and Eastern European beers. Staropramen and Tyskie *were* my favorite beers. Their recipes will most likely change.

Additionally, Anheuser-Busch has a 50% equity stake in Grupo Modelo (Corona, Modelo, and Pacifico). The Craft Brewer Alliance (Redhook and Widmer and partially owned by Anheuser-Busch) holds a minority interest in Goose Island Beer Co. and Kona Brewing Co. of Hawaii. Heineken has a 50% stake in Lagunitas.

The one thing I should clarify is that I do not hate all corporations and chains, and many of them are socially responsible and sustainable. At the same time, there are huge privately owned companies that are just as bad as corporations when it comes to political corruption and pollution. However, so long as a corporation's accountability remains in the hands of a few people who have nothing but profit as their priority, there is very little incentive to be socially responsible, sustainable, and provide quality products and services. If you are going to invest in the stock market, I would strongly urge you to find a socially responsible mutual fund like Parnassus.

Let's talk about PBR for a second. PBR used to be owned by a conscientious independent operator who donated to charity and kept his price low so coal miners or whatever the heck Midwesterners did back in the day could afford it. So during the 00's, hipsters drank PBR, but unbeknownst to most of them, PBR is contract-brewed by Miller-Coors now. Yes, it's cheap and affordable, but so is McDonalds coffee. Drink up.

As far as I'm concerned, **Pigeon Head Brewery**, **Great Basin** and **Silver Peak** have the best micro-brews, because they have the most unique beers that are not all IPAs or Belgians. Like those three, **Brasserie St James**, **Brew Brothers**, **BJ's**, and **Craft Depot** are microbreweries and restaurants. Brasserie has come a long way and is probably one of the four best, but I just hate Belgian beers. Belgium is like the Autobahn, it's just a fast way of taking Germans where they want to go. Brew Brothers is comically unoriginal. **Under the Rose** is a strong microbrewery with a fun tasting room filled with adult games, okay adult-size kids' games. Newly opened in Reno are **Lead Dog** and **Record St.**

Chapel, Imperial, Reno Public House, Craft, St James, Ole Bridge, Waldorf, Duffy's, Lincoln Lounge, Pinon's Bottle Co., The Saint, Brewer's Cabinet, Whole Foods Bar, Mellow Fellow, Beer NV, O'Ski's and most of the Eldorado bars surprisingly have a great selection of beer either on tap and/or in bottles.

Photo: Reno Public House

Besides Rombauer, Renoites have a bizarre fetish for Underberg and now Fireball. San Francisco has a bizarre hipster fetish for shooting Fernet.

Distilleries

Some new distilleries in the area include **Branded Hearts** and **Craft Depot** in Reno and **Seven Troughs Distilling Company** in Sparks. There were no laws governing distilleries in Nevada until Assembly Bill 156 was passed in 2013. Seven Troughs is an exemplary distillery that uses Nevada grain and distills all their liquor onsite. They are sustainable and authentic using pre-Industrial methods for distilling. Since they only recently opened, they do not have any long-aged whiskeys yet, but they do make moonshine, vodka, and rum. They have a tasting room and limited hours Friday and Saturday. An outstanding distillery a bit further away in Fallon is **Frey Ranch Estate Distillery** which has an outstanding vodka.

Where to Buy Liquor and Wines in Reno?

Total Wine has an amazing selection of not only wine but liquor and beer. They say they have 8,000 wines, 3,000 liquors, and 2,500 beers, but that's across all their 80 stores I have to imagine. They also say they're the largest independent retailer of fine wine. It is a staggering display of booze to say the least. I would have never imagined twenty years ago Reno would have a store like this much less a selection of more than 20 beers at any bar. **Ben's Wine and Fine Spirits** has been this town's traditional liquor, beer, and wine purveyor with a surprising wine collection. **Craft** is our hipster boutique beer and wine store where you can shop for beer in a walk-in cooler which sucks in the winter but rocks in the summer. You can also buy any beer or wine there and open it and drink it there. They display all their wines inside their boxes which reminds me of an old wine store, Corkscrew on Arlington which had wine boxes stacked on top of each other, and you'd have to ask the owner where anything was. **Grand Sierra** has a tasting machine. It's pricey as you can easily blow through $40 in an hour, but it does allow you to try some pricier wines without buying the whole bottle and perhaps regretting it.

Whole Foods opened **Tap Room** which is more of an alcohol tasting room than a bar since it closes at 10 PM and the huge windows make it incredibly bright inside. But I do like the way they market regional, craft beers and offer 64oz growlers which are big jugs you can buy and then refill with the beers they have on tap. Very environmental! Just don't start breaking out the 360 IPA. They usual have a nitrogenated beer on draft that makes any beer incredibly smooth and silky. I'm a huge advocate of nitrogenated beer. We used to have nitrogenated Caffrey's Irish Ale in America before MillerCoors ate it and limited it to Canada and Britain. If you haven't noticed, the beer conglomerates like to buy competing beer brands and then stop making it. Or even worse, they change the recipe to create the Bud or Miller version. A few years ago, I ordered a Rolling Rock on tap at Slice and went back to the bar and said, "I'm sorry I ordered Rolling Rock, I think you gave me the Bud." To my shock and horror, the bartender gave me Rolling Rock. Same deal with Red Stripe. With the popularity of PBR, the conglomerates are bringing back a lot of oldies like Old Milwaukee, Rainier, Hamm's, and Genesee Cream Ale.

Notable Bars No Longer Here

Old locals here might get a kick out this list. Just skip it if you're a visitor. It goes back to 1995 when I moved here so don't expect anything REALLY old.

American Bandstand

(now Harrah's Plaza)

I barely remember the place but remember plenty of hotties. Obviously, back in the 80's and early 90's, Reno was stuck in the 50's. Not anymore. With those Baby Boomers all dying off, with more of a 60's crowd at Hot August Night, the 50's is becoming less nostalgia and more like Civil War reenactment. In fact, CalNeva now pipes 80's pop throughout their casino and outside too. 90's music is now considered retro!

Rodeo Rock

Mt Rose St and S Virginia St

Can you say *Urban Cowboy*? Yeah, John Travolta made cowboys look cool and single-handedly started the whole country revival culminating in country bars opening all over the country often taking over closed disco clubs. I remember when really, really hot women would go to country bars, and there is a second revival going on these days with the young'uns disenfranchised by hip hop and hipsters.

Midtowne Market

121 Vesta St

Not only a great restaurant but a cool place to hang out. Without a significant yuppie market, this place I suppose was doomed or just mismanaged.

Del Mar Station

701 S Virginia St

I went here to my first punk rock concert and jumped into my first mosh pit, and I remember the adrenaline rush but also the assholes on the outside who would just shove dudes who were moshing. I remember hearing about Vanilla Ice playing here with his new rock band.

Molly MacGuire's

125 W 3rd St (now 3rd Street Bar)

There aren't many scary bars in Reno, trust me I've been to them all. Some are sketchy and just have a bunch of old, smelly dudes, but some have felons and are truly scary. Molly's was scary! I once ran into this felon with spider tats signifying prison time or something and some peckerwood tat. He was scary. He drank my friend's beer, and my friend was too much of a pussy to do anything about it. The felon asked if I wanted pot then told me to hang on to a handful of weed he just dumped out into my hand. I just put it down on a table and went to the bathroom, but then he grabs me in the hallway and I'm grabbing him back telling him to relax. Damn crazy. But then one time the cast of some Eldorado casino show was there, and they were a bunch of babes from England or something.

Quest

214 W Commercial Row (now 1Up)

I honestly never went inside here. I saw the inside from the outside, and many times, I'd see drag queens walking out of the place. This was back when there was no trench, and Commercial Row was very dark and more like drug row.

Bad Dolly's

535 E 4th St

I never went inside, but it was renown in Reno as the bad lesbian bar that male bouncers didn't want to work at because it made them afraid, very afraid. I can only imagine.

Stock Exchange

535 E 4th St

After Bad Dolly's closed, it became the Stock Exchange, a nice, upscale straight nightclub. This place has changed ownership and names many times since including a short-lived stupid 18-year-old-and-up kiddie club.

Green Room

148 West St (now part of West St Market)

Yes, the infamous Green Room. Green Room was the music scene in Reno. I had many a great memories there including a couple make out sessions.

Peyton Place

1114 E 4th St (now Cadillac Lounge)

I never went inside, but back in the day, this was the swinger's club.

Vino's Italian Restaurant

241 N Sierra St

Oh hell 80's retro. It was like 2006 and I was always amazed at how popular this place was with hot women dancing to 80's pop music. The place was really odd shaped though with a small dance floor in the middle and then booths and tables off to each side. It was a restaurant during the day. The good thing was that when you wanted to sit down and take a break, you could just hang out at one of many empty booths.

Reno Live

210 N Sierra St

There was a time when you had mega-clubs, and there was one in Sacramento in the 90's called America Live. Reno Live was like that, and it had a Top 40's dance club, a country club, a rap club, and downstairs a techno club. Those were the days huh; we all got along, albeit in separate rooms. I preferred the techno room, but there would hardly be anyone there, mostly what looked like under-aged kids who would one day grow up to rule 1Up!

Fritz's

1305 N Virginia St (now Rick's Pizza)

Speaking of underage, I met a few under-aged girls here acting all grown up like they were UNR students. I can only imagine the thrill they had partying with actual college kids and dudes that were much older than that. Needless to say, pursuing 19-year-olds never went very far. Back then, I found out through their MySpace page how old they were.

Amendment 21

425 S Virginia St (now Creazian restaurant)

This was actually a pretty cool place. It was a bar and grill, but they'd have live bands that would get so packed, it would be incredibly uncomfortable and it took forever to get a drink. But then on other nights, it would be totally dead. I liked playing pool here both downstairs and upstairs. And they had Georgette, the hottest bartender in town! Not only that, but she's just one of those people who seem to have an incredible heart. So much good karma. She now works at St. James.

210 North

210 N Sierra St

This club was a game changer. Reno had never seen such an upscale, sophisticated, elegant, beautiful night club. But Reno was just not big enough to sustain it especially after the Great Recession hit.

Peace Café

50 N Sierra St #106 (now Reef sushi)

I really liked the place and miss it. It was hit-or-miss, but they had Latin dance night where I and my friend invented a new drink, half a glass of Shiraz and half an energy drink. It actually tasted great, and we'd drink those before dancing. Peace Café was owned by a group of people with some weird, controversial thing going on. At first, they said that for every meal, they donated a meal to the homeless, and they were very hippie and community-oriented, but then there were accusations of misallocated money and stuff. Some dude bought it and reopened it as Urban Beats but quickly closed it. There were rumors about unknown debts or something.

Divine

95 N Sierra St (now Sticks, formerly Chocolate Bar)

This started off as a really upscale restaurant and nightclub, and I think it intimidated the heck out of Reno, because it was so high-class and Reno didn't have many of these types of places. I think Chocolate Bar when it was on California Ave gets the distinction of being the first in Reno to introduce a sophisticated, elegant, coffee-colored, upscale *Sex and the City* interior design for a bar. 210 North then blew everyone's minds. It was like a club that belonged in Miami or LA. But then I guess college coeds and 20-somethings warmed up to Divine, and then there were freaking lines to get in. Even when you got in, it was like Disneyland, and there was a freaking line to go upstairs where everyone wanted to be despite the fact that there was a perfectly good dance floor downstairs. They took out a lot of the seats and tables to expand the dance floor downstairs. Then tourists got wind of it, and slowly, gradually, the crowds became more and more ghetto, and finally, no local wanted to go there and it just died.

Photo: Divine during the Santa Crawl

1099

1099 S Virginia St (now Chapel)

OMG. This was an infamous everything bar: gay, lesbian, bi, transvestite, transsexual, hermaphrodite, androgynous, you name it, 1099 had it, 1,099 varieties of sexuality. They also had a backroom which I never checked out. I think you needed a secret password or something, and I heard all sorts of shit went on in there. Their Pink parties were usually packed and fun and even had a few hot, straight women.

Chocolate Bar II

13979 S Virginia St, Suite 505 (The Summit)

The original Chocolate Bar where Brewer's Cabinet sits gave Reno *Sex and the City* chic. Chocolate Bar II was an underappreciated masterpiece.

CommRow

255 N Virginia St (now Roundabout and Whitney Peak Hotel)

CommRow was a peculiar bar/eatery/club/concert/recreation/ entertainment complex opened in 2011. They did not get packed except during major bar crawls. There were three bars and a nightclub on the first floor and a bar upstairs next to the indoor climbing boulder park. They re-opened the concert venue called Cargo as well as their 164-feet climbing wall along the outside of the building. 2012 and 2016

91

Libertarian Presidential candidate Gary Johnson climbed all the way to the top. Unfortunately, he never climbed all the way to the top of the polls.

Foley's

3655 S Virginia St (now Lucky Beaver)

Before it moved to across the Atlantis, Foley's was across the Peppermill (now Clary's). Across the Peppermill, it was a cozy bar with a mix of locals and Peppermill tourists. When they moved to the new location, there was a moving party where we helped move everything in the bar that was not nailed down including chairs and tables. At the new location, it lost its cozy charm but became renowned for having the hottest bartenders and waitresses in town.

El Cortez Lounge

235 W 2nd St (now Faces)

Cortez was a dive bar that had karaoke seven-days-a-week that was quite hipster and popular in its days. Cortez witnessed the transition of karaoke from middle-aged, out-of-key crooners to 20-something pop star wannabe's probably a result of the TV show *Glee*. Cortez had one of the most famous or infamous bartenders in Reno, Rudy, who looked like Cheech Marin. He was a hard-working, hustling, traditional bartender who wore a tie and vest. He was the classic cocktail master before it was cool. Before the hipster cocktail revolution he was the only bartender in Reno outside of casinos who wore a tie and vest. Chapel was the second to pick that tradition up. Terry, the bar owner, closed after the Siegel's bought the Cortez hotel and retail space and raised his rent.

Other Bars No Longer Here

Closed: O'Farrell's also known as "the phone booth." Carmel's Pub on South Virginia near Longley which used to be Brewhouse Tavern, Porky's near Mira Loma, Beaches Bar & Grill on South Meadows, a number of Bully's and Sparky's around town that I'm not listing them all, Carl's Pub, Billar de Raza was Breakpoint, Sullivan's Sports Bar & Grill, Dolce at GSR. Atlantis night club, Tubby's Bar and XOXO both on Wells, Stained Glass and Nixon's both on West 4th Street, Carnaval a gay club for a few weeks was Vino's, Urban Beets was Peace Café, the Liquor Box and Desert Sunset Bar both on East 4th Street, Keystone Cue'n'Cushion, Scruples, Good Times, and Morandi's Record Street Brewing Company. Fourth Turn Bar & Grill. Cantina Ruby's Bar. Bella Sera was Placido's was Midtowne Market (a very nice restaurant and wine bar). Confetti's on Grove closed then reopened as a nightclub that closed. Coco Boom split up into a bunch of different stuff and used to be Del Mar Station was Peppermint Lounge was Club-a-Go-Go. Spiro's (Reno) is now part of the Sands parking lot. Harrah's Plaza was American Bandstand. Tronix. Bass was Baseline was Bliss was Masquerade's was Stock Exchange was Bad Dolly's a very bad, lesbian club. Pinup bar at the Bowling Stadium was Bully's was Que'n'Cushion. Good Times. Chocolate Bar II at the Summit. All the bars at CommRow. 775 Gastropub was Bully's (now Cheesecake Factory). Strega. Hawk's Nest. Rise was 210 North was Level was Pacific Beach Club was Metropolis was Reno Live was Eddie's Fabulous 50's casino. Candela. Shorty's was Fat Daddyz. Tronix moved across the street to where Neutron's was and Visions before that. Strega. Giant Dollar Basic was a crazy obscure four-seat bar at the back of a tiny convenience store. Celtic Knot was Napper Tandy's was Revenge Bar was American Bar. GR's Lounge was La Shay Lounge which had a stuck up barfly named Maxine who never talked to anyone. Hamdog's and Mambo's. Ruben's Cantina. Bar USA. Buffalo's Silver Cue Billiard Ultra Lounge was Diamond's was Breaktime Billiards. Se7en was a part of the Green Room. Beach at GSR was Nikki Beach. Hellfire Saloon was the Red Room was Black Tangerine. The Grape and the Grain. Corrigan's. Men Wielding Fire was Club Zulu was Dick and Jane's was Rodeo Rock. Rock Bar was Knitting Factory was Rocky's (casino and bar). Se7en at West Street Market. Val's Midtown Lounge.

Bar changes: Shea's Tavern was Duncan's Pub was Seven Fifteen Bar. Smokin' Bully's on Wedge Parkway was Timberline. Flowing Tide 3 was Spiro's Sports Bar and Grille. Bangkok Cuisine 2 was Sage Creek Grill & Taproom. Key Club was Penthouse was Goldfinger strip club. The Wild Orchid strip club was Discopolus. The Loving Cup was Biggest Little City Club was Satellite. Jub Jub was Broken Spoke was Stoney's. Foxy

Olive was the Lamplighter Lounge. 3rd Street Blues was Blue Lamp was Molly MacGuire's, one of the scariest bars in Reno. Tonic was Blue Lamp too. 1Up was Wurk was Red Martini was Quest and a liquor store. West Street Market was Cadillac Lounge. West Street Wine Bar was part of Liquid. Cadillac Lounge was Peyton Place. Fantasy Girls was Fantasy Ed's. Spice House was Diamond Jack's was Spice House. Lincoln Lounge was Jazz Club which was not a jazz club was Davis Bar. Corkscroo was Breakaway. Moxie's on Caughlin Parkway was Café Soleil Bistro & Wine Bar was Hilltop. Brewer's Cabinet was the original Chocolate Bar. Chapel was 1099. Clary's was Foley's was a holding jail. 40 Mile Saloon was the old Chapel was Mr. O's was Eddie's was Office Bar was Dunc's. The Point moved from W 4th St to S Virginia. The W 4th St location used to be a gay bar called Reflections and then a straight bar, Summit Saloon before that. Joe Bob's on Mill was Crazy Weiner's Sport Bar. Lucky Beaver was Foley's was Stinger's Bar & Grill was Tailgate was Sunset Bar & Grill was Hooter's. Mixers was Russo's. Pub was the Fish Bowl at the Peppermill. Flowing Tide bought both Reno and Sparks Sparky's. Our Bar was The Bar. Boots and Daisy Dukes at the William Hill Sport Book at the Grand Sierra was Xtreme was Pearl Ultra Lounge was All-City was The Garage. LEX was Mustang at GSR. NoVi was Bubinga. Sneaker's was Harry's All American Bar was Harry's Watering Hole. The Jungle was Jungle Vino. Coach's #2 was Spitfire was Sparky's. Flowing Tide was Sparky's. Man Cave was Ace in the Hole was a Green Bay Packer's bar. The Stick was Chocolate Bar was Divine Club. Mellow Fellow was Slice. Knockouts Sports Bar was Scurti's. Liberty Food & Wine Exchange was Reno Provisions. The Rack was Fallout Shelter was Woolworth's. Knockouts was Scurti's. Rick's Pizza was Wolf's Den was Fritz's. Faces was Trocadero was El Cortez Lounge. BlueBird Nightclub was PB&J was Bodega Club was Club Underground was Ark-A'ik. Headquarters was Singer Social Club was Club Babylon. Blind Dog Tavern was Monolith Bar was Ampersand was Whisky Bar was the original Se7en Teahouse and Bar. Jimmy B's was Murphy's Law Irish Bar was Money Bar was Murphy's Law Irish Bar was Black Horse. Upscale Lounge at Creazian was Amendment 21 was Scampi was Adele's. Hard Water House was Joe Bob's was Sonny's Italian.

In Sparks, closed: Roper Dancehall & Saloon, Playhouse Lounge, and Jib. Bar Code was Donley's Irish Pub. Lupitas Bar was Buckin' Wild Dancehall & Saloon. Trader Dick's at the Nugget. The Mad Hatter. Cat's Meow at Bourbon Square Casino. Anchor's. CBQ Cowboy Bar & 'Cue was Cadillac Ranch. Gilley's at the Nugget.

Changed: Paddy'n'Irene relocated down the block. Blitz was 50 Yard Line Bar & Grill. Mummer's was Alley was Vixen. Morelli's G Street was

Robin's Nest. Bottom's Up was Road House Saloon. O'Cleary's Irish Pub was Rack'n'Pinz at Legends. Bottoms Up was Road House Saloon. Sparks Lounge was Sidelines. Oak Tavern was Aspen Glen. Flowing Tide was Sparky's. Millennium was Oasis.

Elsewhere: McHenry's Pub & Grille in Spanish Springs closed. High Desert in Stead closed. Lemmon Lounge in Lemmon Valley closed. Pour House in Golden Valley closed. Desert Winds Beer & Whiskey Bar in Raleigh Heights. In Sun Valley, JR's was Call of the Wild and Kelly's Bar was Harvey's Sun Valley Bar. Stumpy's Pub in Sun Valley closed. Mudslinger's was Spurs Saloon was Lonestar Saloon.

What I Learned From Hitting Every Bar in Reno

Bear with me, I've included this cute, little story I wrote in 2011 about my experience trying to hit every bar in Reno:

I learned that my liver is in serious trouble. I learned that I'm a raging alcoholic with no life and no conventional, meaningful aspirations in life. Okay, I already knew that. It all started last winter on a cold, drunken night, the start of most interesting stories in my life. My friend from the Midwest was bragging about hitting all the bars except three in some college town out there. We had no idea how many bars there were in Reno, so the next day, I tried to find out, and I learned quickly it was a son-of-a-bitch chore-and-a-half. First, there's no list out there. So I compiled the list from the Yellow Pages book, online Yellow Pages, and Google maps, and even then, I wound up with an incomplete list that included a butt load of old, closed bars. But then it dawned on me, how exactly would you define a bar?

We had another meeting and came up with this definition based simply on the goal of having fun and not wasting our time sitting at a stupid, lame bar. A bar is a place that serves alcohol to people who party there on a Friday or Saturday night and spend the majority of their time drinking, listening to music, dancing, or getting lap dances and not gambling, eating, or bowling. Even though many places have "bar" or "pub" in their name, if most people go there to eat, it doesn't count. Blind Onion Pizza & Pub doesn't count while Pub & Sub does. Even Brew House Pub & Grill didn't count even though they have both "brew" and "pub" in their name, because most people went there to eat. Now you could split hairs with any of the Bully's Sports Bars out there, but we agreed that they're bars, and loads of people go there on Friday and Saturday nights to party and just drink.

We also agreed that a self-contained party venue at a casino like Edge or Brew Brothers counts while the Silver Baron Lounge doesn't, even though most people there are not gambling. If you count Silver Baron Lounge, then you'd have to count the cabarets at Peppermill and Atlantis, and the heck if I'm spending a Friday or Saturday night at those cabarets. No offense to those who do and enjoy the old people music that is suspiciously beginning to sound like the music I grew up with. I counted Roxy's Lounge while we didn't count Rapscallions or Vivoli that also have live music, because I don't think people just go to Rapscallions or Vivoli's for the music or drinks whereas many people just go to Roxy's Lounge for the music and drinks. I imagine some lawyer could argue technicalities and demand that his client's bar be counted on our list, but no such lawyer contacted us.

After wading through all that shit which was an on-going process of refinement and tedium, I came up with 160 bars. As we worked our way through the list, however, it went down to 138. I also learned that I had been in Reno way too long. I came up with a list of 80 bars that had been closed or renamed in the last 15 years.

I also divided up the bars by regions and learned that Reno really doesn't have well defined regions like Manhattan or San Francisco. On my list, there was Stead, North Valleys, NW Reno, Old South Reno, South Reno, Far South Reno, East Reno, Midtown, Wells Ave, Downtown, East 4th Street, and University.

Another thing I learned was that there is a shitload of new bars in Reno. 58 of the 138 bars on my list opened within the last five years. When I first moved to Reno in 1995, I used to tell people that the only young, single women lived in Sun Valley, and they had four kids by five different dads, which doesn't make any sense, but you try explaining that to the kids. Things all changed in 2005. Too bad it took ten damn years. That was my lost decade I guess. I'm not a studly, charming, handsome, young buck anymore, not that I ever was, but I'm certainly wiser and more devious than my young competition now.

We, as in me, the Midwesterner and her fiancé, started out with the goal of hitting 100 bars, but I hit that on Christmas Eve, and to my shock, those fucking drunks were closing in on me fast. I mean I've lived here 15 years, and they just moved here two-and-a-half years ago. I thought I was a bar crawling boozer.

Time and time again, I've been surprised at how nice and friendly the bar patrons of Reno are. I hit a few bars on my own. On Christmas Eve, I was three bars from hitting 100. I decided to finally check out Fat Daddyz the scary-ass looking bar on East 4th Street just west of the US 395 bridge that always seems to have Harleys parked outside. There was only a bartender and a woman inside playing pool, and although the bartender looked like a tough biker dude, he was real cool. There was also a nice collection of photos of women's boobs adorning the wall above the bar and what looked like a new collection of women's asses. I couldn't help but recall that whale's tails are all unique and can be used to identify them and women's boobs seem to be too, because I'm just a weird fuck who thinks up shit like that right.

I then hit Alturas, another biker-looking-bar that I had avoided, until I went inside, saw the t-shirts up on the ceiling and realized that I had been there before. That happens sometimes. The bartender was even friendlier, and she even introduced me to a group of friends at the end of the bar and told them I was trying to hit 100 bars in Reno. A funny thing happens when you tell people this, they immediately ask, "tonight?" Yeah, I'm going to have 100 drinks in 100 bars in Reno tonight. I think it's one of those reactions like when someone tells you they're a pilot, and you react, "Oh, you fly planes," and they're like, "No, I fly horses. I jump on them, they sprout wings, and off I go, on my fricking Pegasus to Narnia." It's funny, but they quickly realize it's 100 bars over a longer period of time.

The group at Alturas was then kind enough to all accompany me to Cadillac Lounge, and yes, Cadillac Lounge became my 100th bar in Reno. I'm not one of those gay-phobes or gay bashers. I support gay rights a hundred percent, and straight people are increasingly hitting up gay bars, especially straight women. Maybe it's a nice break from being hit on all night long or simply the better dance music. Seriously, what's up with that? I always worry about being hit on at a gay bar, but that's probably a bit presumptuous of me, although I have been two times. It's funny to notice that when a dude hits on you aggressively, he comes across as pathetic and desperate while when he does it more like a casual friend, he seems more respectable and cool. I should learn from that, but I continue to hit on women aggressively and probably come across as a total pathetic and desperate creep, yay me. Like I'll ever run into them again right?

In the end, there was one of the Alturas gang left, and he took me over to Dilligas, yes Dilligas, Dilligas, that place, you know, that place, on East 4th Street, THAT place, wink wink, nod nod, say no more. Okay, the swinger's joint, there said it. Cadillac Lounge actually used to be Peyton Place, the other infamous swinger's bar, but I had been to neither. I did try to get into Dilligas once, but it was couple and members only, but I didn't realize that it's only that way on Friday and Saturday nights. This was Thursday night. We both got in easy, and the bartender was even kind enough to allow us to tour the back room. I'm not sure if they want to be known as the swinger's bar, maybe the lifestyle alternative club that may or may not involve varying levels and types of consensual sexual arrangements or something? The fact that there's a metal gate door for the back room makes it look like a dungeon, but inside, it's just one big sofa, cushion lounge thing with some sort of construct in the middle where it looks like you could tie someone up and spank them to your heart's content, although, why anyone would enjoy being tied up and spanked is beyond me. I imagine somewhere a dude's getting off being water-boarded, placed in stress positions, having women's menstrual blood smeared on his face while a German Shepherd barks at him and someone takes his photo. I imagine Rumsfeld explaining, "Torture?

Torture? I do that shit every Friday night with Cheney. He loves that shit. He'd tell me if I was being too hard. We have a safety word, 'Hilary.' Boner disappears, I stop immediately. We got W Bush in on it once, but that sick fuck started to creep the shit out of us."

The next week, I proudly announced to my friend that I had hit 100 bars in Reno, and she thought it was cool, and then she changed the subject. I don't know what I was expecting a trophy or some big fanfare or Reno Council Medal of Honor. I kept prodding her about when she was going to hit 100, so about a month later, she decided to hit all the bars in Stead. Unfortunately, as with all her concocted bar crawls, she planned to do it in costume, the Stead Snuggies Bar Crawl. Okay, first of all, yes, Snuggie? As in the blanket with sleeves because you're too lazy to pull your arms out from under your blanket to change the channels using a remote control?

Yeah, and of all places, Stead. Seriously? If I'm going to hit up some dive bars in Stead, at least I want to be able to zip up my back side right. Another thing I learned was that, at least in Reno, the bars are not nearly as pants-crapping, scary in the inside as they look on the outside. I always fear the Eddie Murphy moment in *48 Hours*. I fear walking into a new bar, and the music screeches to a stop and everyone in the bar turns around and stares at me - because I'm so hot, yeah, that's right, because I'm so dang hot. Fortunately, that moment never happened. To my continued surprise, people in Reno bars are pretty cool and friendly. I've heard stories of people getting chased out of Midwestern and Southern bars. Maybe it's because Reno is a transient town with not many regulars. Maybe it's because people out West (and east of California) are just more open-minded, friendly, and cool. As a Westerner, I'm naturally biased, but does anyone else think East Coasters and Californians are uptight assholes?

We hit Hangar Bar, High Desert, Sneakers, Spurs Saloon, and Lemmon Lounge and had a great time, and the people there were nice and friendly. Of course, we also had three dudes 6'4" and over and two of them were big and muscle-bound. That always helps, and we also had more women than men, so the bar patrons certainly could not have minded that. But even if I just went alone, I think there would have been no problems, unless of course, I went alone wearing nothing but a Snuggie with an open backside for convenient crapping.

I'm not sure when the whole costume bar crawl thing became so popular. The Santa Crawl hit Reno five or more years ago. I remember first seeing about forty of them on East 4th Street, and now it's almost everyone downtown. I believe it started at Abby's. My friends from the Midwest used to do costume bar crawls when they lived there. I get the sneaking suspicion that there's not much to do in the Midwest besides drink, farm, procreate, attend college games, and make exquisite gem sweaters. Besides the Santa Crawl, Reno never had any big, organized ones until recently with the Super Hero and Zombie Crawl and the short lived Turkey Crawl. Yeah, dressing up as an American Indian may not have been totally PC especially when you live in a place that has a reservation in the middle of its city. I Googled Santa Crawl, and there was Santarchy as early as 1995. But now, you see small birthday party groups all dressing up like in 70's or 80's retro themes. My friends love dressing up. It takes effort just for me to dress up for Halloween and work. But after two or three drinks, I don't mind, but I will draw the line at women's clothes and walking around topless or that new thing, the no pants parties not that there's anything wrong with dudes wearing women's clothes or people who like to walk around in public without any pants.

I also remember when Abby's had a vintage fire engine they used as a party bus. My friends got this old 70's RV and converted it into the ultimate party RV complete with an artistic paint job on the outside. They also collect bumper stickers on the back, and they accepted my Sierra Club sticker but rejected my NRA sticker. Seriously? Damn hippies. The party RV is so anachronistic, it's timely. But this is not a party bus or van like the Amendment 21 party bus, a mere transport vehicle between bars. They stock up the fridge with booze and sometimes an extra tub with ice, and they park it near bars, but you can just hang out and party there most of the night, and it winds up being a lot cheaper too. They have a disco ball inside and a PA where they heckle and tease people passing by and sometimes invite them in. Yeah, the single women or pair of women almost never take up the offer. We did have one dude join us and suck down ten beers. I think he might have been homeless. It's such a new strange, concept, I think most people think the RV owners are a bunch of weird, old hippies and they're surprised when they enter and the owners are both in their twenties along with most of the party folk inside.

I told this one dude that it was sort of like that candy wagon in *Chitty Chitty Bang Bang*. But instead of luring children with candy, the party RV lures adults with a hippie looking exterior and alcohol inside. And like the candy wagon, the walls would come down to expose a metal cage that would cart the victims off to some dungeon. He left soon after.

One of the bars we missed on the Snuggie Crawl was the Wayside in Lemmon Valley, so a couple weeks later I decided to go back and check that off my list. I was a bit leery of this joint from the outside. It was late at night, and when I walked in, there were three dudes: a bartender who looked like a biker with a motorcycle t-shirt, a guy with a cowboy hat at the bar, and another guy at the bar who looked like a trucker. Living in

Reno, you think it's a small city, but when you go out to Lemmon Valley and drive back into Reno, you start thinking, wow, I'm hitting the big city with all the bright lights. I ordered a beer and decided to take off after one, but the bartender offered me some taco soup. I had never heard of it and imagined the basic ingredients of a taco thrown into a soup. I said no thank you, but he insisted. He told me his mother made it, and it was sitting in a crock pot. So he got some out, heated it up in the microwave, put some cheese and Fritos chips on it. It was really good, and when I asked him how much it was, he said there was no charge. That was probably the best, most enlightening moment I had hitting all the bars in Reno. A lot of us "city folk" think we're so open-minded to diversity and live with people from all over the world, but then we cling to this preconceived notion that all rural folk are closed-minded and bigoted just because they don't live with people of different races or nationalities, but that's not why they live in rural areas. Sometimes, it's all they can afford, or they just prefer a more laid back lifestyle. But when you compare the hospitality of big city bartenders and patrons to rural bartenders and patrons, I have to tell you, it's the big city bartenders and patrons who seem more closed-minded, unfriendly, unhelpful, snotty, and xenophobic. If you live in a big city, sure your taxi driver may be from Pakistan, you may have a Vietnamese dry cleaner, and an Estonian doorman, but are they your friends? You ever invite them over to a party? Sure, you patronize them with small talk, but you keep them at arm's distance, because you fit into another class. How open-minded is that? And don't get me started on the fact that most gay and racist jokes I've ever heard come from big-city comedians not rural people.

Reno, of course, fits somewhere in between a big city and a rural town. But it's not just our size. We are truly a unique city of newcomers. I don't think people here have figured out where they fit in yet or even if they fit in Reno at all. You think you're walking into a dive bar, and you'll run into young 20-somethings or a city councilmember. You walk into a gay bar, and you run into straight people. You'll find blue collars in a wine bar and burners with hula hoops in a sports bar. Okay, probably Mexican bars are the exception to the exception. We hit up Coco Boom, and we were the only non-Mexicans there, but none-the-less, we were literally treated like VIP's and had a great time. Reno folk are ever moving, ever experimenting, ever adapting, morphing into any scene, valuing both the old and the new, the strange, the scenesters, the outcasts, barbies, preppies, hipsters, whatever, people with no names or groups. Who cares if corporate media reinforced by Reno 911 considers Reno some trashy, sleazy, trailer city podunk? By fault of being worthless in their eyes, Reno becomes cool, at least with hipsters who think anything mainstream media thinks is not cool is by default cool. I guess my fear of entering a hostile bar is the fear of not fitting in anywhere, but the fact that nobody really, truly fits in around here makes this one of the easiest places to fit in. Basically, in Reno, you can be whatever the fuck you want to be in addition to doing whatever the fuck you want to do. I mean seriously, you can have sex for money and gamble legally here while smoking medicinal pot balancing on an exercise ball and call it palates if you want. You can also try to hit every bar in Reno and realize most of the time you're just like everyone else, being somewhere you've never been before. I think between creating the list and finishing it, several new bars opened and several closed. My next goal is to hit every bar in Sun Valley and Sparks, and I think after that, the novelty will wear off or I will just die of liver disease.

(Or write a Reno travel guide)

The Obscure Reno Art Scene

The Salvagery - 2530 Wrondel Way (formerly 900 E 4th St)

Arts and event space home to several Artist Collectives and the 2011 Burning Man Temple of Transition project.

Generator, Inc. - 1240 Ice House Ave, Sparks

Community art space with a lot of Burners

The Potentialist Workshop – 836 E 2nd St

Performance art theatre

The Holland Project – 140 Vesta St

All-ages art and music showcase for young people

Morris Burner Hotel - 400 E 4th St

Hotel for Burners and Burner venues

Nada Dada - (motel locations change each year)

Open art showcase started in 2007 at the El Cortez Hotel (hotel rooms converted into art studios) as an independent counterpoint to the tightly controlled Artown Festival in July.

Valley Arts Research Facility - 420 Valley Rd

Rents space for artists, hosts gallery shows and inexpensive concerts for mainly local bands

Fort Ryland - 243 Ryland St

Basement of a house, live music venue

Mountain Music Parlor – 735 S Center St

Folk music workshops and concerts

Picasso & Wine - 148 Vassar St

A combination wine bar and painting workshop venue

Dr. Sketchy's Anti-Art School - (various locations)

Live model (as opposed to dead ones) sketching and drinking. As my friend Leslie told a news reporter, "I tell my friends, 'I'm going to drink and draw tonight.' They say, 'What?' 'Don't worry about it. I'll be fine. It's totally different. Drink and draw, not drink and drive.'"

What are Some Good Special Events?

Year Round

First Thursday at Nevada Museum of Art

First Thursday of each month, the museum has a nice party between 5 PM – 7 PM where you pay $10 to get in and can check out the art and get some booze and listen to the live music. Unfortunately, the two hour event is way too short to make it much of a party.

January/February

Chinese New Year

Chinese New Year is not January 1. It is sometime in late January or early February depending on some complex algorithm. It changes each year, but they celebrate the 15 days after Chinese New Year's Day. Downtown Reno casinos are transformed into Chinatown with more Chinese people in downtown casinos than the entire Reno-Sparks metropolitan area. If you love Chinese food, culture and people and the little kiddies and the little, old Chinese ladies, then you'll love just hanging around the casinos during this two-week festival.

February

Mardi Crawl

Basically dress up in beads and a purple shirt, and you're good to go. A new bar crawl with promise.

Sierra Arts BrewHaHa at the Nugget

This is a beer festival that raises money for the Sierra Arts Foundation and offers a large selection of beers to taste. Back in the day, I swear, the selection sucked, but fortunately times have changed and you'll find more and more independent breweries.

Valentine's Pajama Crawl

Coinciding around St. Valentine's Day, this bar crawl is new and steadily gaining popularity. Used to be a vampire crawl

Rotary Club Mardi Gras Food and Wine Tasting

The Rotary Club just started this great wine and dine Cajun festival. Reno really doesn't celebrate Mardi Gras, so this is about the only time you get to wear beads and show off to old dudes from the Rotary Club. Unfortunately, they celebrate on Tuesday. Who the heck goes out to party on a Tuesday? Next year, I'm taking Wednesday off. I'll probably say that every year and never go.

Jack T. Reviglio Cioppino Feed and Auction

This event has spanned over three decades in Reno and raises money for the Boys & Girls Club of Truckee Meadows. What is Truckee Meadows? It's one of many names for this area that includes Reno-Sparks, Reno-Tahoe, Washoe County, Sierra Nevada, and Great Basin. Jack T. Reviglio was a local who was one of the founders of the Boys & Girls Club which is a safe and affordable place for youth age 6 to 18 to hang out. Cioppino is an amazing fish stew created in San Francisco, kind of like paella minus rice.

March

Leprechaun Crawl

There's nothing like drinking all night on a Sunday, Monday, Tuesday, or Wednesday and then going to work hungover. For this reason, we now have a St Patrick's Day theme bar crawl the Saturday preceding St Patrick's Day.

St Patrick's Day

If the weather is good and it's a Thursday, Friday or Saturday, it feels like the whole city comes out for St Patrick's. The main center of festivities used to be Wells Avenue with all their Irish bars, but it is now transitioning to Ceol. It's not as big as New Year's or the Santa Crawl though, and the weather usually sucks.

April

Yuri's Night

This party is usually held around April 12, the day of the first manned spaceflight by cosmonaut Yuri Gagarin. It really has little to do with that event but rather an excuse to party in primarily Burner theme with interactive Burner art showcases, playa atmosphere and music. This is Reno's biggest Burner event of the year usually held at BlueBird Nightclub (formerly PB&J).

University of Nevada, Reno Alumni Association Beer Festival

This is a beer festival that raises money for the university alumni association. Not sure what they do with the money, but who cares really, it's a beer festival with a great beer selection and raffles.

Big Chefs, Big Gala (formerly Spring Splendor, formerly Grand Chef's Gala)

This is a fundraiser for the Big Brothers Big Sisters of Northern Nevada. Of course, our fundraisers are not on par with big cities like New York or LA, but they are the big social scene here for the generous. Our fundraisers usually charge between $50 and $150 per individual with $1,000 to $2,000 tables. In New York you're paying $1,000 a plate and $10K+ for a table. In Reno people actually bring real dates not escorts. And as with all fundraisers I guess, everyone is old and gets their photo taken for the "scene" page of some local magazine. **Sean Savoy** and **Isha Casagrande** probably have the Reno record for most scene page appearances and are our local big socialite celebrities.

April - September

Reno Aces Baseball Season

I rarely know what our standings are, who's on our team, what's on third, and often I leave before the end of the game. Why do I go? There's something cool about going to a baseball game, eating hot dogs, and drinking over-priced, shitty beer from a plastic cup. It has something to do with America or something. This stadium is small, so you can get pretty close to the action and lots of homeruns landing on the heads of unfortunate homeless people across the tracks.

May - October

Reno Street Food

Every Friday, food trucks, misc. vendors, and a band converge at Idlewild Park. It used to be located at CitiCenter but the Food Truck Friday folks had a meltdown when these guys started using the same venue on other Fridays and caused a big scene and then no longer had a food truck event there anyway. Don't you hate that?

Feed the Camel

Every Wednesday, there is a food truck festival under the Wells Ave overpass behind the McKinley Arts Center. You park at the McKinley Arts Center.

Sparks Food Truck Drive-In

Food trucks and a free movie at the Victorian Square amphitheater.

May

I'm not mentioning Cinco de Mayo, because we don't really do much. A few casinos have festivals in their parking lots, but I'm thinking, if I want authentic Mexican food, there's a taco truck down the street. The Mexicans don't even celebrate Cinco de Mayo. That would be like us celebrating February 18. What's that? The end of the War of 1812 against Britain, duh. Even Andrew Jackson didn't know that, and he was in the war, and funnily enough, if he had known it ended on February 18, he probably would not have become President and made it to the $20 bill.

Reno Fur Party

You know it's springtime in Reno when it's 80 degrees one day and the next it snows. You also know it's Spring when the Aces start playing. You also know it's Spring when the Fur Party comes around, held now at BlueBird Nightclub. This is another semi-kinda-Burner affair as fur has become fashionable at Burning Man, however partiers wore fur at Berlin's Love Parade before Burning Man. Just FYI.

Reno River Festival

After spending a long miserable winter suffering, Reno comes out to play around the river and celebrate warm weather although sometimes it actually snows in May. Good excuse to day drink and wear your favorite wife beater and child molesters (short shorts, I know this will never catch on). Bring your sunglasses though, because all of Reno is still pale from the winter.

June – August

Farmer's Market at Sands Regency Hotel Casino (parking lot south of the tracks)

Sparks is perhaps the most boring city in the universe after Chernobyl, okay before. The Rib Cookoff is the only reason to go there, and now with the Farmer's Market moving to the Sands, pretty much stay on I-80 if you have to travel east of Reno. Instead of raising revenue through business sales from special events, they get most of their revenue from traffic citations.

June

Epic Fandom Crawl

This is a new umbrella category crawl for nerds and geeks which includes subsets of Cosplay, Comic Book superheroes, Sci-Fi, Fantasy, video games, etc. Basically, if you're dressed up as anything, you won't stand out.

Reno-Tahoe Odyssey

If you have twelve friends who want to relay jog 178 miles around Reno and Lake Tahoe over a 24-hour period, not only do you have a bunch of very healthy friends, but you have a bunch of very healthy crazy friends.

A Toast and Taste of Summer Wine & Food Expo

Featuring 20 area restaurants and 40 wineries and breweries, this is an Encore Beverage fundraiser for a designated charity each year.

Street Vibrations Spring Rally

This was Street Vibrations 20 years ago before all the gangs turned it into some Vendettapalooza™. (I didn't really trademark that term, although I should.) This is a very small event in Sparks, but you can actually enjoy being a biker and hanging out with mellow bikers not gangs. You can even ride your Japanese bike to this event and not be bullied or laughed at.

Reno Rodeo

Okay, so I'm not country, cowboy, or anything like that, but it doesn't matter. The Reno Rodeo attracts everyone: city slickers, Latino migrant families, UNR students, everyone. It's a fun, festive event with beer gardens and carnival games. A great place to take a date. And if you have a cowboy hat, it's the only place besides a country bar you can wear it without getting mocked. Seriously, I wore my cowboy hat into Harry's one night and this Native American wanted to fight me, I'm not kidding.

Nada Dada

Nada Dada is Reno's counter-culture rebel art movement. Reno needs originality badly. The Reno art establishment created this Cow art rip off from Chicago where we had sheep everywhere painted by different artists. We were acting like sheep, ironic. Then it ripped off New York's piano thing where they placed pianos all over downtown. Hello? Originality? Heard of it? There's a great New York Times article on Nada Dada at:

http://www.nytimes.com/2009/06/22/us/22reno.html?_r=0

Eldorado BBQ, Brews, and Blues Festival

You can get slammed at this event. You buy a pass and fill up at several beer stations and also stuff your face with BBQ ribs and pork sandwiches. A typical S Virginia St downtown festival that is fun for all. This doofus Reno News & Review writer once criticized Reno special events as magnets for trailer trash, but every special event in any big city attracts the masses, and there's nothing wrong with poor people, get over it. Reno has this inferiority shame complex about poor white people. I'm sorry but I don't recall folks on the Mayflower or at Ellis Island being royalty.

Reno Rockabilly Riot

I attended my first rockabilly concert at Speakeasy about ten years ago. I was truly impressed at the details of both women's apparel and hairdos. Not sure how popular it is now but popular enough to close off streets downtown.

July

Artown

The entire month of July is Artown with an amazing assortment of art events every single day. This is perhaps Reno's greatest invention and the best time to visit Reno. The weather is almost always awesome, not too hot and never muggy, and it often cools down at night.

Chicken Wing Cook-Off

Not as big as Sparks' Rib Cook-Off but slowly gaining popularity in downtown Reno.

Reno Basque Festival

If you didn't even know there were Basque people, you might want to check out this food and music festival at Wingfield Park.

July 4th Sparks

Sparks always has a great July 4th festival with a very long fireworks show, however, be prepared because the place gets jam packed along Victorian Ave and parking's a bitch. When I was a kid, fireworks lasted ten seconds, and we just threw old WWII ammo up in the air. These days, midway through the show, I'm like, seriously, seriously, I have to go to the bathroom. I go back to O'Ski's and get another beer, come out, still going.

POPS on the River

This is the Reno Philharmonic Orchestra's big annual fundraiser. It's best to buy a table, that way you can dress up in theme, decorate your table, have food catered, and get closer to the orchestra. There are contests for best costumes and table themes. Invariably, they pick recent movies as themes or just weird stuff like Alice in Wonderland, pirates, Egyptians, *Reno 911*. The music is mostly Broadway.

Super Hero Crawl

Dress as your favorite super hero, villain, or just make shit up like many people do. Captain Douche Bag? Slightly Racist Dude? Cosplay Dude Who Obviously Thinks a Super Hero Crawl Includes Cosplay? Supergirl If She Was a Hooker?

August

Hot August Nights

They say this is the largest classic car festival in North America and probably the world unless you count the entire nation of Cuba which uses classic cars year round. It is also Reno's largest special event. There used to be a 10 PM curfew downtown with Israeli Defense Forces (RPD) guarding against potential terrorism (mass ethnic assembly).

Pirate Crawl

Those crazy bar crawl folks keep changing the dates around. This used to be in September then moved to July and now August. Dress up like a pirate and go to bars downtown. This bar crawl is slowly getting popular.

Oh, you have no idea what it's like being the only one dressed up as a pirate at a bar. I'm telling you, being an innovator isn't easy.

A Taste for Art

The Nevada Museum of Art puts on this annual fundraiser to support their education and exhibition programs. They have wine and food pairings and of course art.

Best in the West Nugget Rib Cook-off

I've avoided this festival until recently when I finally realized it wasn't all that bad and over-rated. When they put the BBQ on fire, you must realize, smoke gets in your eyes. I'd bring along those wet-nap packets too.

Reno Gay Pride Festival

Yes, Reno does have gay folk. The only way you'll ever get to listen to decent electronic dance music in public.

Burning Man

This is not in Reno, but it's always fun to watch all the burner vehicles come to town and buy up all the water bottles at all our local grocery stores and then afterwards watching the carnival of dust-covered vehicles. Some burners then have decompression parties afterwards throughout Reno. People think burners are dirty, smelly homeless hipsters, but they're actually dirty, smelly dot com millionaires and Bay Area doctors and lawyers. Nothing like getting legal advice at a Burner camp from a naked attorney from San Francisco which I did.

September

Street Vibrations Fall Rally

Unless you're in a bike gang and your chapter President requires you to go, I'd skip this one out. In 2011, the Hells Angels and Vagos got into it killing one Hells Angel.

http://archive.rgj.com/article/20130801/news/130801009/Watch-video-brawl-sparked-Nugget-shooting

I've seen shooting videos before, and you'd think everyone drops and takes cover, but you'd be amazed the number of people who just mill around not sure what the hell to do, even walk right into the shooter.

Also, if you drive around Reno, half the bikers either don't obey the law or can't ride, so you have to be extra careful. They also tend to ride in packs, so good luck merging into their convoy. You pretty much have to wait until they all pass until you can switch lanes. Every year, at least one biker crashes and dies. Worst thing is in the morning, if you sleep in, you'll get woken up by all the loud Harley tailpipes.

I think they finally killed La Tomatina en Reno, because this was one fricking lame event. First of all, once again, good 'ol original Reno rips it off from some other city. Second, it's a huge waste of food, and there are people starving in Nevada. Third, who the frick wants some asshole throwing tomatoes in your face? I think at the end, they should scoop up all the tomatoes and put it on a big pizza and eat it. It embodies the worst of Reno: unoriginal, uninspired, copycats, wasteful, and thoughtless.

October

Eldorado Great Italian Festival

This is the last big downtown festival of the year, and it's so sad. I often go just because I keep saying I'll check out a festival during the summer and never do, so this is my last chance to be an honest guy, well somewhat because it's not in the summer. It's actually a nice food festival where you can pick a bowl of pasta and then pick any sauce from several vendors. Just get here early before they run out of everything. Eldorado's mushroom ravioli is to die for. Do not do the grape stomping contest. I did this with my friend one year, and besides homoerotic undertones, I had to throw away my shirt and jeans.

Zombie Crawl

Basically wear a coat of white base paint, then put black stuff around your eyes, have fake blood dripping from your mouth, and dress up as anything you like and you're good to go. I hate this crawl, because I always look stupid in makeup. I look more like a Panda bear than a zombie.

November

Barrels & Bites (formerly Vintage Nevada)

Southern Wine & Spirits is a major liquor distributor here in town and showcases all their booze and over 500 wines to benefit a local charity. One of these years, perhaps AA? Every year, they have more cognac, Scotch, whiskey, bourbon, rum, tequila, and vodka. This is THE premiere alcohol festival in Reno. It is like Christmas, Thanksgiving, Valentine's Day, St. Patrick's Day, and New Year's wrapped up in a few hours of blacked out bliss. One of my favorite black-out events in Reno.

Fantasies in Chocolate

This is Reno's largest black tie party. Of course, many Renoites don't know what black tie means and show up in suits or sport jackets. Oh well. It's Reno's biggest pompous affair, but a great excuse to shove five pounds of chocolate down your gizzard and hit on women suffering endorphin seizures.

CanFest

Most people think that beer in a can is cheap, corporate stuff like Hamm's, Olympia, Miller, Steele Reserve 211, Four Loko. But increasingly, breweries are discovering the benefits of cans. Not only is it cheaper to transport, but it preserves the beer significantly better than bottles, even brown tinted bottles. And if you are a true beer connoisseur, like me, you pour your beer into a glass anyway, so who cares if it comes from a can or bottle? The only real issue is BPA in the lining of any can.

Onesie Crawl

Formerly a pajama crawl, this has become hugely popular as more people feel comfortable in onesie's than random pajamas.

November - February

Rink on the River outside Aces Ballpark

It's not Rockefeller Plaza, but this is our nice little outdoor ice-skating rink.

December

Santa Crawl

Not sure if this was an offshoot of Santarchy which happens around the world, but this is Reno's biggest bar crawl full of people dressed up as Santa or other Christmas related icons.

New Year's Eve

Most cities, you celebrate New Year's in a bar, but in Reno, you can stand in the middle of Virginia St and hug and kiss everyone.

Special Events No Longer Here

Safari Club Convention

Safari Club moved this annual event to Vegas. The only reason you would attend this event, unless you were a prostitute who wanted to hook up with rich dudes from New Zealand, Australia, and South Africa, was to eat the wild game they killed. LaStrada, Prime Rib Grill, and Bistro Roxy all had special Safari Club menus to die for (well, the animals died for). They had alligator, ostrich, buffalo prime rib, boar, and all sorts of exotic stuff you'll never find anywhere else, unless you wind up in a zombie apocalypse and have to resort to ransacking a zoo.

Photo: wallaby says, "Well, I wasn't planning on this trip to Reno either."

Nevada Day Governor's Banquet

Governor Sandoval created this event in 2011 to benefit victims of the Reno Air Races crash and Carson City IHOP shooting. On September 6, 2011, a nutcase walked into IHOP and randomly killed four people including three Nevada National Guard soldiers. Sandoval made it an annual event to celebrate Nevada Day which is October 31, the date Nevada became a state in 1864. Our state slogan is "battle born" as we became a state during the Civil War on the Union side. We should actually be called "politics born" as we quickly became a state to include our vote in the 1864 presidential election. This would be like Obama making Puerto Rico a state to win the 2012 election. Nevada sent 1,200 men to the war, however, not to kill Confederates but secure the Western frontier. More significantly Nevada contributed $400 million in silver which is about $5.5 billion in today's dollars. The feds take our silver, our land, our taxes, our soldiers, and what do we get in return? The highest unemployment in the union because of a financial crisis in which the feds aided and abetted Wall Street robber barons.

Where to Gamble and How to Beat the System?

I'm honestly not much of a gambler. I want the huge payouts like $250K or $1.5 million; hence I play Wheel of Fortune or Megabucks when it goes above $12 million. I used to play a little Blackjack, Craps and bet on the field, and then Roulette and bet on black or red, but after witnessing a streak of 14 reds and 00's and betting on black four times in a row, I realized, even trying to play the odds, you'll get screwed. There actually is only one way to beat the system, but it takes a lot of self-discipline, and like all gambling, it can get addictive and you can wind up losing in the long-term.

You walk up to a bar with video poker, put in $20, order a drink before playing (you will get a free drink every 45 minutes), tip the bartender, and in two hours and 15 minutes, you will come out either even or ahead depending on what you usually drink. In Vegas, you break even after one-and-a-half hours. The question is, can you make your $20 of video poker last two hours and 15 minutes? On top of this, do you want to waste two hours and 15 minutes just to get free drinks? Personally, I'd rather talk to people and pay for my drinks. If you tip $2 a drink, the bartender will make your drinks stiffer and you'll break even sooner. In order to make your video poker game last, forget the straights and flushes and go for three-of-a-kind every time, and throw away useless hands.

Downtown Casinos

Eldorado - 345 N Virginia St at 3rd St

The Eldorado, Silver Legacy, and Circus Circus are all owned by the same corporation and physically connected by large skywalks. Eldorado and Silver Legacy are large, nice, classy casinos. Circus Circus not so much. They should really blow up the pedestrian walk between Circus Circus and Silver Legacy. Eldorado has solid restaurants: La Strada an Italian place, The Prime Rib Grill, and Roxy.

Silver Legacy - 407 N Virginia St at 4th St

Open in 1995, this is still a pretty nice casino with a monstrosity of some ugly, iron, silver mining contraption in the middle of a huge dome. It is the ugliest, weirdest-looking thing you've ever seen. Silver Baron Lounge is in the middle and used to be a prostitute grotto.

Circus Circus - 500 N Sierra St at 5th St

It's not actually that bad, but not exactly my scene. They also have this huge carnival game, circus, arcade thing with hourly acrobat shows. The games are very hard to win, of course. There is one game where I can beat the system but the heck I'm sharing my secret and have them take it away.

Harrah's - 219 N Center St at 2nd St

Harrah's is the third nice, large casino downtown. Lack of a large nightclub kills their nightlife. They have Sapphire Lounge, but this place is small for a nightclub and has never done well consistently. They newly opened The Stage @ The Zone but um, forgot the dance floor.

CalNeva - 38 E 2nd St at Virginia St

CalNeva is a large casino that has that old, 70's charm and is very popular with locals and the blue collar tourist crowd. When I first moved to Reno, I often went here. They also have karaoke where you are literally crooning to the ENTIRE casino floor! I like to imagine myself as some old-fashioned cabaret singer. They also have popular albeit popular-last-decade beer pong tournaments on the second floor of the east building with hot blackjack dealers in skimpy attire.

Little Nugget - 233 N Virginia St between 3rd and 2nd St

As the name says, it is little, but it is also not related to John Ascuaga's "big" Nugget in Sparks. I like going to Little Nugget and imagine that I'm back in the 70's or 80's.

Siri's Casino - 241 N Virginia St

Opened in April 2014, the newest casino in Reno with a Miami South Beach, art deco theme.

Sands Regency - 345 N Arlington Ave at 4th St

Sands is a medium-sized casino that has a summer pool party that attracts a few hot, bikini-clad babes and hundreds of horny dudes. There's a bikini contest where some contestants are strippers and strip down to pasties. Think about it, they can win $500 for three minutes of work or get maybe $10 in tips for dancing on stage at a club for ten minutes. With Nevada regulators cracking down on casino pool parties, the contests may not be around much longer. The former Sands President Ferenc Szony used to star in the weirdest local TV commercial ads. Once he dressed up as the mother from *Psycho*. His son is actually a very talented local artist.

Casinos Elsewhere

In local newspaper survey after survey, Peppermill and Atlanta rate the highest in customer service. Since they're not downtown, their strategy is providing excellent customer service, especially to locals. It also helps that they are privately owned.

Peppermill - 2707 S Virginia St

Peppermill recently expanded and has become the largest, Vegas-style casino resort in town. I truly have to applaud their renovations, although they did not allow a bus rapid transit station to be built outside their casino. They have an Italian theme, and yes, there are bus stations in Italy.

Atlantis - 3800 S Virginia St just south of Moana

I hardly go here since there is no nightclub or nightlife, but it has been kept up well.

Grand Sierra Resort - 2500 E 2nd St just east of US 395/I-580

Anchored by LEX now, this casino has redecorated twice as the GSR and worked hard to improve the place. This venue began life as the MGM Grand in 1978 and boasted one of the greatest shows on the planet "Hello Hollywood Hello." In 1985 they sold and became Bally's. After Bally's parent company went bankrupt, they sold for $83 million to the Hilton in 1992 which invested an additional $86 million. Caesars took over Hilton's gaming division and sold the Reno Hilton for $151 million to GSR Corp in 2006. GSR Corp additionally invested nearly $100 million into it but failed to make a payment on its loans and sold to the Meruelo Group in 2009 for only $42 million. They invested $25 million into it as well as adding LEX which cost $14 million.

Nugget (Sparks) - 1100 Nugget Ave (partially under I-80) just west of Pyramid Way

Most Sparks locals go here and it gets tourists for big events like Hot August Nights, Street Vibrations, or the Rib Cook-off.

There are other casinos about, but they are too far out of town to get any attention from me. Or you have this local casino chain called **Dotty's** where they cater to locals, and it's like your neighborhood casino. I guess it's doing well, because they've opened a bunch of them recently. Great idea for those who like to gamble close to home. One notable large casino is **Fandango** in Carson City which I just discovered!

Casinos No Longer Here

Again, this only goes back to 1995. You can read more about really old casinos in Dwayne Kling's book, *The Rise of the Biggest Little City: An Encyclopedic History of Reno Gaming, 1931 – 1981*. There's another book called *Reno-Tahoe Country: An Illustrated History* half of which seems like an advertising section for local companies.

Fong's New China Club

This closed way before 1995 but I've added this one, because it's kind of cool. Bill Fong was a Chinese dude if you could have guessed, and he ran a casino that allowed non-white's when most major casinos did not. Fong established the first local scholarships for black students.

Harold's - 234 N Virginia St (now part of Harrah's outdoor Plaza)

They had a huge, ugly, old western mural on their wall. It was demolished in 1999. American Bandstand nightclub was located inside this casino.

Eddie's Fabulous 50's - 45 W 2nd St (became Reno Live, 210 North, then Rise, then closed)

It was full of 50's crap. The dealers used to wear those huge poodle skirts.

Reno Hilton - 2500 E 2nd St (now Grand Sierra Resort, formerly Bally's Reno and MGM Grand)

The general layout of the Reno Hilton was about the same as the Grand Sierra Resort, except, there was much more going on downstairs in their mini-mall area. They used to have a movie theater that eventually became a budget, discount movie theater with independent films and big films after a year or so. I fondly remember watching *Run Lola Run* there. They also had weird love seats instead of conventional movie seats. There was also a large arcade. There was also an annual convention of sex or nudists where I heard they had nude bowling. From 1978 to 1989 at the MGM then Bally's, Reno had the largest stage show in the world, "Hello, Hollywood, Hello" with 142 performers. They still have the mini airplane prop behind the stage. Reno probably had four great eras, the 30's, the 50's, the 80's, and the 00's. The book *Dancer's Reunion* by R. Douglas Johns seems like an insider's look at the showgirls of "Hello, Hollywood, Hello," including real photos from that era.

Flamingo Hilton - 255 N Sierra St at 2nd St (now Montage condos)

They had the best grand entrances with loads of neon and then neon flamingos all along the wall. They had a free show with three or four dancers on the casino floor with a decent, albeit nasally singer who belted out Broadway tunes. I remember one time this mentally deranged dude went up near the stage and placed small candies on the stage for the dancers. Fricking Reno. The Flamingo closed in 2001.

Speakeasy - 590 Lake St at 6th St (now Reno Regency Apts.)

My friend used to work here. They had what were probably the first and only raves in Reno with mostly underage kids. I remember walking around and seeing some teenager with butterfly wings practically in her underwear.

Fitzgerald's - 255 N Virginia St (now Whitney Peak Hotel)

Fitzgerald's came alive for St. Patrick's Day. They had this big, ugly leprechaun at the main entrance and in the front, slot machines with like 98% payback which they said was real, but then they also say most people don't cash out when they're ahead, so practically it's not like you sit there and put in $100 and get $98 back, you most likely put in $100 until over time you just lose it all. They had three floors with the buffet and an Irish bar on the third. They closed in 2008. I went there the last weekend and sat at the cabaret bar acting like a wistful fool. I've learned that as you get older, you don't go visit places right before they close. Remember them in their glory days not their last days. Not sure that can apply to humans.

What Are Other Attractions in Reno?

Theaters/Theatres

Pioneer Events Center - 100 S Virginia St

Well, it's not Broadway, but it's the closest Reno gets. It also includes concerts, operas, and ballets for the old folk. It's where all our old lawyers, doctors, and casino owners hang out.

Brüka Theatre - 99 N Virginia St

Independent, local theatre company in a medium-sized, cozy theater. I went there also for a hypnosis show that was amazing. I am a believer in the power of hypnosis. I was put under hypnosis on stage. I never thought it was possible, but I realized later that a good 20 minutes of time had simply disappeared. I have no idea what I was doing. This hypnotist, Dan Kimm is also a therapist, and in the end, he gives you some pretty inspirational guidance that I honestly believe helped me in my life.

Good Luck Macbeth Theater - 713 S Virginia St

They say they do classic work but despite their namesake they do not always do Shakespeare and some "classics" can come from the 80's.

Reno Little Theater - 147 E Pueblo St

Museums

Nevada Museum of Art - 160 W Liberty St

The first Thursday of every month, they have a party with live music from 5 to 7 PM.

Terry Lee Wells Nevada Discovery Museum - 490 S Center St

This is a children's museum and what I like to call an exploratorium although that does kind of sound odd and if the kids have too much fun it becomes a vomitorium.

Sierra Arts Foundation - 17 S Virginia St #120

This is a small gallery on the ground floor of the Riverside Artist Lofts, a building that used to be a casino hotel and converted into lofts specifically created to house artists.

Liberty Fine Art Gallery - 100 W Liberty St

Stremmel Art Gallery - 1400 S Virginia St

Sheppard Fine Arts Gallery, University of Nevada - 1664 N Virginia St

National Automobile Museum - 10 S Lake St

Bill Harrah, the owner and founder of Harrah's, had an awesome car collection he turned into a museum. If you like old cars, this is your museum. If you like old oven mitts, this is not your museum. Harrah also owned the Rancharrah, a 150-acre sprawling estate with horse stables and a gigantic mansion even by today's standards. It was sold in 2015 and converted into a master planned community. Ranch-Harrah get it? Great wealth like this reminds me of the scene in Schindler's List when Schindler wonders how many more lives he could have saved by selling a few more luxury items. Imagine the lives Harrah could have saved or improved selling a few of his acres or cars.

Zoos

Animal Ark - 1265 Deerlodge Rd

This is a wildlife sanctuary for "non-releasable animals" and open to the public. I guess prisons are for non-releasable humans. It's 25 miles north of downtown Reno and also gives you a good look at our desert sagebrush landscape. I'd 4-wheel it in the winter.

Recreation

Grand Sierra Arcade and Driving Range

Whether you're an adult who enjoys golfing, trying to nail a few islands on an artificial lake, or a kid who likes to play video games, laser tag, climbing walls, and a VIP party room for your birthday, Grand Sierra is for you! They also have bowling lanes. There's also a 180-foot thrill sling shot thing that shoots you over to Sparks.

Reno Arch - 255 N Virginia St

Yeah, everybody goes to the Reno Arch to take their tourist photo. Here's a piece of advice: Don't stand right under the arch. First of all, you'll get hit by a car, and second of all, you'll be so small, nobody will recognize you. Stand about 60 feet back from the arch on the sidewalk and then have the photographer place you nicely right under the arch. These days people do crazy things with landmarks like lick them, sit on them, or lean against them. Put your arms out like you're holding the arch up.

Reno's Other Arch - 1 S Lake St

This is Reno's original arch from 1927 and was on Virginia Street until it was redesigned in 1963 and then replaced in 1987 by the cheesy, Disneyland sign up there today. In 1995 it was taken out of storage and placed on Lake Street. It gained local notoriety in 2010 after some sexy Hong Kong celebrity, Rosemary Vandenbroucke, drove her RV into the sign returning from Burning Man and possibly still high off her ass.

Whitney Peak Hotel (formerly CommRow) - 255 N Virginia St

Photo: formerly CommRow outdoor climbing wall

There is boulder climbing on the 2nd floor, and you can with some certification, climb the outside wall all the way to the top of the hotel. I plan on doing this someday. Someday. Right?

National Bowling Stadium - 300 N Center St

If you're into bowling like Woody Harrelson in *King Pin*, then you'll want to check out this bowling mecca. You have to be in a tournament to play here.

Safe Shot Indoor Range – 9425 Double R Bl

8K sq. ft. indoor range and 7K sq. ft. retail gun store. Rent guns to shoot including full auto machine guns. With the recent accidental death of a shooting instructor at the hands of a 9-year-old, I have to warn you that short-barrel, full auto guns flip upwards due to weight distribution. You need upper body strength to keep it under control. I personally don't believe kids should fire either full autos or high-powered weapons that only teach them to flinch and become poor shots.

Sparks Marina Park - 300 Howard Dr, Sparks

The one Reno-Sparks park I will mention is this big lake. It's a two-mile jog all the way around including the mini-peninsula in the middle. It used to be a mining quarry they filled with water and fish (I'm assuming they put the water in first). It's actually the nicest park in the area, and in the summer, they have boat rentals, scuba diving, fishing, windsurfing, sailing, and swimming. There is a bar in the complex adjacent to the lake. Then you can walk through a parking lot to get to Sparks Legend, a big retail, restaurant complex.

Wild Island – 250 Wild Island Ct, Sparks

Large water recreation park including a huge slide, wave pool, bowling lanes, bar, mini golf, and go karts.

Grand Prix Go-Kart – 6895 Sierra Center Parkway

50,000 sq. ft. indoor go-kart racing facility. Adult carts reach 45 MPH.

IMAX Theatre at Galaxy Luxury+ Theatres at Legends, Sparks

Reclining seats, beer and wine available, and ginormous state-of-the-art screens

Tommy's Grandstand Grill & Deli – 830 Meredith Way, Sparks

Five automated batting cages, two automated golf driving ranges, four private tunnels, video arcade, grill, and deli

Sports

Reno has minor league baseball (**Reno Aces**) and D-league basketball (**Reno Bighorns**). Former NBA protégé Jeremy Lin used to play for the Reno Bighorns. **Nevada Wolf Pack** football is probably our most popular sport. The Nevada Wolf Pack basketball team actually used to be pretty good and made it to the Sweet Sixteen in 2004 but not any longer. We used to have a minor league hockey team (Reno Renegades). Mixed Martial Arts is popular in Reno with non-UFC leagues. **Ryan Bader** grew up here and **Page VanZant** started training MMA in Sparks. **Gina Carano** is related to the Carano's that run some of the casinos here and attended UNR for a year. Reno also has roller derby (**Sierra Regional Roller Derby** which now includes **Battle Born Derby Demons**) which now has a male skater. The big sport in the area is obviously winter sports at Lake Tahoe. Reno now also has a professional minor league soccer club called **Reno 1868 FC** (Football Club).

Where to Shop in Reno?

Well, that all depends. If you're looking for high-end shopping, you might not have wanted to leave Northern California. We have **Dillard's** (Summit Mall), **Macy's** (Meadowood Mall), and **Nordstrom Rack**. We have a number of high-end boutiques at **Summit Mall**, our high-end outdoor mall way south of Reno at the intersection of I-580/US 395 and Mt. Rose Highway. It's twelve miles south of downtown Reno. **Meadowood Mall** is our indoor mid-end mall. You can find the youthful, fashionable discount store **H&M** there. We used to have a Parklane Mall, but that was bulldozed. There is **Sparks Legend** a few miles east of the Sparks Nugget (aka downtown Sparks). It has a bunch of high-end outlet stores, but not many. You can find the other youthful, fashionable discount store **Forever 21** there.

There are nice high-end boutiques dotting the rich parts of town like far Northeast Sparks and far South Reno. There are also high-end boutiques dotting Lake Tahoe where multi-millionaires both live and play. Isha Casagrande opened **The Coutoure Closet** on Plumb and Arlington. If you're into mid to low-end shopping, Midtown has a dozen nice boutiques and secondhand fashion stores. One notable store is **Plato's Closet** which sells second-hand designer clothes. The owner happens to be our new mayor, **Hillary Schieve**.

There's a bunch of notable hippie/hipster/vintage/burner/dress up stores in town:

- **Melting Pot** - 1049 S Virginia St
- **Junkee Clothing Exchange, Inc.** - 960 S Virginia St
- **PolyEsthers Costume Boutique** - 655 S Virginia St
- **Hippies** - 1921 Victorian Ave, Sparks

For rockabilly/pinup style clothing:

- **Dressed Like That!** - 711 S Virginia St

If you're into sporting goods, we have two government-subsidized monstrosities, Scheels at Sparks Legend which is like Disneyland for the outdoors and Cabela's next to Boomtown about nine miles west of Reno on I-80. We also have **Patagonia**'s headquarters and a retail store at 130 S Center St.

What are the Top Ten Things to Do Around Reno?

There's a www.10best.com website that lists 10 attractions in Reno: Mount Rose, Nevada Museum of Art, Nevada Discovery Museum, National Automobile Museum, Rancho San Rafael Park, Truckee River Whitewater Park, Riverwalk and Arts District, Reno Arch, Idlewild Park, and UNR. That list is pathetic. Idlewild Park? Seriously? It's a fricking municipal park. That's like saying, go to LA and go to MacArthur Park. Why? To feed the ducks? I can do that at home. You go to a city and do stuff there you CANNOT do at home. Go to Reno and check out McDonalds! So here's my list:

1. Take them to Lake Tahoe

Seriously, unless it's snowing, drive them 36 miles to Lake Tahoe taking I-580/US 395 south and then Mt. Rose Highway west. Mt. Rose Highway is super winding, so be careful. I'd take US 50 back to Carson City then I-580/US 395 north back to Reno, because I don't like using up my brake pads going down steep mountains, and it's also easier to die if you slip off a big drop. Plus, you can wind up behind some asshat doing 20 MPH, because they're even more afraid of dropping off the side of a cliff. Plus, you get to drive through old Carson City, the state capital. What do you do at Lake Tahoe? I don't know, ski, snowboard, sit on the beach, hike? I just like going to the casinos at Stateline on the south side. During the summer and winter, they have a great nightlife scene especially with all the well-to-do Cali-tourists who go there to ski or snowboard in the winter or vacation in the summer. Part of Lake Tahoe, Squaw Valley's Olympic Village is a pretty good-size, upscale shopping, hotel, condo, dining district. In 1960, they hosted the Olympic Winter Games.

As the rich get richer and the poor get poorer, I'd like to take the opportunity to impart on people just how wealthy the Bay Area has become. It is the premier tech center of the world in a tech era. There are 56 billionaires in the Bay Area. If the Bay Area was a country, it would be ranked fourth in the world for number of billionaires. But forget about the billionaires. The average salary at Google is $141K. This includes janitors and receptionists. Keep in mind, this excludes stock options, and many smart workers including Zuckerberg will take a $1 salary to avoid paying payroll and income taxes and get paid in stocks. Lake Tahoe is the playground to some of the wealthiest people in the world. You have no idea.

2. Take them to the downtown casinos

The major casinos to check out are Silver Legacy, Eldorado, and Harrah's. The rest are a little rundown and local, but then again, if that's your cup of tea I'm not knocking it. I enjoy hanging out at some dive casino sometimes, CalNeva being my favorite. You can also go all out and take them to a casino show. It won't be Vegas with like 20 dancers, more like a dozen if you're lucky, sometimes several, but they're much cheaper than Vegas. If you have time, I would also suggest Peppermill which now reminds me of a big Vegas hotel resort.

3. Take them to the West Street area

This is a great, compact area full of not only bars and restaurants but little boutiques shops, and its down by the river too.

4. Take a walking tour of Midtown

Midtown generally starts with Cal Ave to the north and goes all the way down to Plumb Lane and then basically Wells Avenue is the western border and Holcomb to the east. They plan on renovating Virginia Street around here, and if all goes to plan, this place will be one awesome pedestrian area. Right now, the narrow sidewalk throws you out into on-coming traffic.

5. Take them to LEX at GSR

In previous editions, I suggested taking them to strip clubs, but I don't think some people appreciated the humor in it, and I'm not sure if Wild Orchid, Spice House, and Fantasy Girls still have the pass deal where you get into all three clubs for $25. A huge Vegas-style club may not be your cup of tea, and you may not enjoy the TSA pat down before entering, but aren't you just a little bit curious? If I could go back in time, I would have killed to go to Studio 54 or even a French aristocratic ball. You don't have to pay $50 or wait two hours in line to see what a Vegas-style mega-club is like and generally the EDM music they play. It's just one of those things that are iconic of this era that will probably go away with the next generation.

6. Hang out at bars and clubs until the sun comes up

Why? Well, first of all, it's just damn fun, but second of all, you run into all sorts of crazy characters, and once in a while a stripper or two. Here's a list of some 24-hour bars on Friday and Saturday nights: Doc's, Jox, Shea's, Alibi, and Bully's. Coach's, Tonic, and 1Up are open way, way late. Most all the casino bars are 24 hours. Keep in mind, you have to start drinking at 11 PM.

7. Take them to Burning Man

It's 120 miles north of Reno, why not. But isn't it this weirdo, freak show, hippie, hipster, naked drug fest? I wish. You know where I can find that and what camp it is? They did a survey at Burning Man, and low and behold, bunch of middle-aged, college-educated rich folk. Gee, with $500 tickets, wonder why? However, you don't just go to Burning Man like you go to Disneyland. You have to prepare like you're going on a three to ten-day camping trip. There is no going in and out of Burning Man and staying at a hotel in Gerlach the town nearby. My only year there, I stayed in a tent with a tarp on top, and by 8 AM, it was way too hot to sleep. Do not lash your tent to your car thinking you're all smart, because the winds will whip your ropes into your car paint.

The city is only like two miles across, and I can easily walk that in New York City, but in the hot sun, walking on soft sand, and under the influence with little sleep, trust me, don't walk, take a bike and a lock too. Burning Man is like taking shrooms I hear. If you want it to be a wonderful, spiritual, religious, adventure, it will be. If you want it to be a few hours of stark raving madness and paranoia, it will be. Don't expect. Chill out. Don't be self-conscious. Chances are, half the people feel just like you, looking around, wondering what to do, how to pose, how to approach people, what to say, etc. Just be there. Also, if you bring a tent, seal up all the mesh, because the sand storms will leave a layer of sand all over your shit. Maybe leave the zipper door slightly open, because I'm sure if you seal plastic up, you'll suffocate.

Also, read the guide, because I swear, I tried to improvise, but it's very intimidating just walking into some strange camps. The guide tells you where all the activities and camps are. When I travel, I like to plan out a few things and then improvise. Trust me, you'll get a lot more out of Burning Man picking a few things to do each day. Walking around drunk is only fun for so many hours. And then go to Reno to decompress, but don't forget that you don't trade the bartender a pot cookie anymore; you're back in the real world Burner geek. If you're too much of a wimp, at least check out all the Burners at the decompression parties the week after at Sands and GSR.

8. Schedule to take them on one of Reno's Great Bar Crawls

Here are the best Reno bar crawls from the best first: Santa Crawl, Zombie Crawl, Superhero Crawl, Leprechaun Crawl, Pirate Crawl, New Year's Eve, St Patrick's Day, Onesie, and our monthly downtown Wine Walk. The most important thing to remember here is that it's not about the drinking as much as it is the watching. Don't bitch that you can't get a drink because all the bars are packed. Drink ahead of time or stash a flask or detour to a bar or casino that is not on the bar crawl. The whole point is watching everyone else drink and cavort and smile and have a great time. And start early. Usually, the party doesn't start until 10 PM, but for these crawls, all the people in Reno who don't usually come out drinking start around 8 PM. And most importantly, dress up. Not dressing up, I guarantee you, you will feel like the outcast.

9. Take them to a brothel

Okay, seriously, seriously? Okay, I'm not saying partake of their services, but just go to find out what all the nonsense is about. I mean come on, why not? Then for the rest of your life, you can tell people that you went to a brothel. While they don't want people just looking, there's no law against it, and you can just pretend like none of them suit your tastes or you got cold feet and chickened out. You can just sit at the bar and drink, so it's not that weird. With all of Dennis Hof's self-promotion, I think the **Bunny Ranch** is overshadowing the **Mustang Ranch**. Either way, check them out.

10. Take them to Virginia City

After much thought, I added this one. Virginia City is 26 miles southeast of Reno taking US 395 south then Highway 341 (Geiger Grade Road). Virginia City is a total time warp. It has wooden plank walkways and old saloons and looks like the old West. Being mainly a small tourist town, the locals are friendly. More than that, back in the day, there were a bunch of hippie communes out this way. It's not entirely my cup of tea, but it is one of the things that makes the Reno area extremely unique and interesting. And who can go wrong with a bar named the **Bucket of Blood Saloon?**

What is the Weather Like in Reno?

Basically, it's dry. We're 4,500 feet up some mountain range, but it's called high desert. Wrap your head around that, a desert 4,500 feet high. This means two things. First, we're 4,500 feet closer to the sun, so wear organic sunscreen. Second, at 4,500 feet anywhere on this planet, it will be colder than at sea level, so keep a coat handy. You can always tell the tourists in the spring and fall freezing their butts off in t-shirts and skimpy dresses at night. Summers here are almost perfect just find shade to avoid sunburn and keep in mind, except perhaps two months out of the year, it gets cold and chilly at nighttime. Springtime, some get allergies here from sage, but otherwise, not many allergy sufferers here, although in 2017, usually a tree allergy sufferer, I experienced allergies here for the first time probably because of all the rain in the winter. Springtime is something crazy here. It can be 70 degrees during the day, then a storm will float in and it will snow at night. Fall time is the same way. Often it just goes between winter and summer and forgets spring or fall.

Winters are, in my opinion, unbearable with 20 to 30 degree nights. Sometimes it dips below 10. I know I'm a wuss. It snows a little but rarely sticks for more than a week. It gets very windy from time to time. When it does get windy, it gets fricking windy. Also, when the wind blows, it blows sand all over the place so you'll find a nice coating of sand all over and inside your car if you leave your windows cracked open.

As for the dryness, especially in the winter, moisturize, moisturize, moisturize. Your skin will crack and bleed like you have the plague or just turned into a zombie. Get a humidifier, use distilled water, run it once a week, and use bleach to clean it so you're not spewing bacteria or fungus all over yourself and your bed sheets. Avoid medication that dries your throat out, because bacteria and viruses love dry throats. Before I realized this, I spent entire months with sore throats hacking away as if I smoked three packs a day. Oh and seriously, don't smoke, not only does it already dry you out, dry your skin and make you look a decade older, but in Reno, you'll get sick more often. The lack of humidity however makes summer nicer and winter less unbearable.

What are the Hotels Like in Reno?

Photo: Silver Legacy

First of all, keep in mind house or condo rentals, because a friend of mine got this amazing penthouse condo at Park Towers with a 180-degree view that was cheaper for two couples than getting two rooms at a hotel. There is also **Airbnb.com** which hooks up homeowners with vacation renters. With that said, Reno hotels are relatively cheap. The only four-star room in my opinion is the **Summit at Grand Sierra** near the airport and now **Renaissance** downtown. Now keep in mind, the GSR has regular Grand Sierra rooms that are 2.5 stars in my opinion, so make sure you're at THE SUMMIT at Grand Sierra. There's some Hyatt place by the airport I've never been to called **Hyatt Place**. So what's the difference between a Hyatt Place and a Grand Hyatt or Hyatt Regency or Park Hyatt? Park Hyatt is the top level, Grand Hyatt next, Hyatt Regency next, then Hyatt Place. Hotels just add stuff to their names like Courtyard Marriott, Holiday Inn Express, Hilton Garden Inns. I think a good rule is that if they add something weird to their names, it's not as upscale as the name by itself. **Courtyard by Marriott** opened in downtown Reno.

Besides THE SUMMIT and Renaissance, I'd recommend the **Eldorado**, **Silver Legacy**, or **Peppermill**, all solid 3.5 stars. The **Sparks Nugget**, **Harrah's**, and **Atlantis** all are decent 3 stars. Most of the time, on a Friday or Saturday, you can expect to pay about $100 a night or more, and then on Sunday through Thursday, rates are cut in half, seriously. I love Hotwire.com and Priceline.com, and I have landed $35 rooms at

Eldorado and Silver Legacy tax included (plus their stupid resort fees and the $2 bowling tax). In Reno, rates go up in the summer and go down in the fall and spring and nose dive in the winter. Many Renoites will simply get a hotel room for Friday or Saturday night. Think about it. You pay $50 for a hotel room versus paying $25 for a taxi to get downtown and $25 to get home.

Keep in mind, we now have resort fees and a $2 downtown improvement tax to remodel the Bowling Stadium. Go to **www.resortfees.com** to find out how much the resort fee for each hotel is not only in Reno but Vegas too. Keep in mind, they don't update it regularly. Our resort fees go from $5 to $10 as opposed to Vegas where it's more like $20 to $30 a night, seriously. Keep in mind our hotels get booked solid for Hot August Nights and to a lesser extent on New Year's Eve.

Speaking of maids, you better tip them if you're staying multiple nights. They will scrub the toilets with your toothbrush if you stiff them. Okay, probably not, but who's to stop them right? I tip $2 for anything up to $100/night hotel.

Reno does not have any youth hostels. If you can't afford the nicer casino hotels, there are many cheaper casino hotels and cheap motels. Don't forget the plethora of couch-surfing websites out there. It's not as creepy as you think.

Also consider an unusual, eclectic, bohemian night at the **Morris Hotel**.

How Do I Get To and Around Reno?

If you're coming from Northern California, you probably want to take I-80, but there's another more scenic route, US 50 that hits South Lake Tahoe first if you also want to see Lake Tahoe. Keep in mind, during the winter time it can be a downright bitch traveling on either routes with mandatory chains. US 50 and other highways around Lake Tahoe can close altogether. Chains suck. You can hire some dude to chain your car up or freeze your rear off doing it yourself and invariably screwing it up so it's too loose. Check the weather over Donner Pass and Truckee (not in Reno). The reason Reno is a high desert is because the rain and snow get blocked by the mountains, so there could be a blizzard over the pass and it could be sunny in Reno. I just wouldn't drive over the winter.

Flying is very cheap especially with **Southwest Airlines** that does not list themselves on all the major travel search websites. Southwest Airlines also happen to have the best customer service and do not charge you for two checked bags. There is only one major airport in Reno, **Reno-Tahoe International Airport (RNO)**. Why is it International? Because we have flights to Mexico now. The airport is literally inside the city. It is four miles from downtown Reno. We used to have our own airline, Reno Air, but it went down in flames and by the end, I swear every other flight I was using a free travel voucher because of some mess up on a previous flight. I imagine at some point I could have just kept on traveling for free indefinitely, but then again, that's probably why they went out of business.

There is no real traffic in Reno, although, our regional roads and freeways seem to be in a perpetual state of repair or expansion. Behind gaming tax, speeding tickets through work zones is our second highest form of tax income. It takes about 15 minutes to get from downtown Reno to Sparks or anywhere in the McCarran Loop and often beyond.

There are two freeways that each bisect the city, Interstate 80 running west and east connecting downtown Reno with "downtown" Sparks (basically Sparks Nugget) and also Sparks Legends. US 395/I-580 runs north and south. Virginia Street also bisects the city running north and south at a weird 22° angle and eventually meeting up with US 395/I-580 at both the north and south ends. 4th Street used to be the old Highway 40 and goes west to east and connects Reno and Sparks but then becomes Prater Way in Sparks. Unfortunately, for whatever reason in Sparks you'll hit every red light on Prater Way.

If you're only planning on staying in downtown Reno with possible ventures within the city, it may be worth your while not to rent a car and rely on cabs, **Uber**, or **Lyft**. As of July 2015, ridesharing became legal in the entire state. I have taken both Uber and Lyft and would highly recommend them.

Taxis are relatively inexpensive in Reno, and they all speak English. I am serious! I'm not being racist. If you come from a big city, you will experience the odd culture shock of white people serving you everywhere in Reno. If you fly in and stay at the major casinos, most of them have their own shuttle vans. If you are downtown, I'd suggest taking Lyft to check out Midtown and the Peppermill. We have two taxi companies, **Reno-Sparks Cab** at 775-333-3333 and **Whittlesea** at 775-322-2222. I prefer Reno-Sparks Cab. We also have a few limo companies including **Bell Limo** at 800-235-5466 (800-BEL-LIMO).

Also, for all you out-of-towners, it is legal in Nevada to make a right turn on a red light so long as you make a complete stop. It is not legal to run people down as they are walking in a crosswalk. With half the people in Reno coming from California, I would warn all pedestrians in Reno to be careful.

We have electronic meters downtown, and parking is free after 6 PM and on weekends and holidays. There are vacant parking lots downtown which are NOT free. I'm sure some people make more money towing vehicles from their vacant parking lots than if they put any real businesses there. All casinos downtown have free parking except Eldorado which has validated parking. There is also a paid parking gallery with an entrance and exit on W 1st St between Sierra St and West St. The National Bowling Stadium also has a parking structure that charges for special events and Aces ballgames. Also keep in mind, when the Aces play ball, a lot of free parking lots charge $5 to $10.

We do have a 24-hour transit system that is clean and safe called **RTC RIDE** which also runs the Bus Rapid Transit (BRT) line called **RTC RAPID** from downtown Reno to Meadowood Mall at pretty high frequency and Route 1 connects Reno and Meadowood Mall and runs 24 hours. Both these lines travel along Virginia and will hit Midtown, Peppermill, Atlantis, the Reno Convention Center, and Meadowood Mall. Download the app **NEXTBUS**. It has real time arrival information for all routes. It is so frickin cool. You can see the bus actually move up and down the streets. I actually used it when all the taxis were busy for St Patrick's Day, and I only had to stand in the cold for a few minutes. I wish I had this when I took the bus on a regular basis. You can also download the app **Token Transit** to pre-purchase a bus pass. In downtown Reno, there is **RTC SIERRA SPIRIT** a 25-cent/ride electric bus that goes from UNR down to Liberty St from 7 AM to 7 PM and runs every 15 to 20 minutes. The downtown transit center is located at E 4th St and Lake St and is adorned with an old impaled bus. Alternate modes of transportation are definitely gaining popularity especially with the hipster crowd. When I was growing up, only kids rode their bicycles and nobody wanted to admit they took the bus which was often dirty and filled with scary people. Today, it's cool to ride your bike to the neighborhood café or bar. A lot of buses today are larger, nicer, and cleaner and the more regular people ride, the less you notice the occasional drooling drunk. We also now have a huge migrant working population that relies on buses.

Walking between downtown and Midtown is easy just stay near Virginia Street. You can rent a bicycle at **Sands** casino, and increasingly we have more and more bicycle lanes, but bicycling along Virginia Street is still not safe. We passed a new law that requires cars to give bicycles three feet of room when passing, but yeah, like people will actually do that. You can rent a ScooterBug motorized personal mobility device at **Eldorado**. I heard in Vegas, people without mobility challenges ride these around. We don't have any mules or horses to rent, although you can rent a motorcycle with **Adventures of Reno** at Grand Sierra or **Harley Davidsons**. There is a helmet law in Nevada which is kind of odd since you can legally have sex here with a prostitute and bet a corporation that a ping pong ball will land on a number between 1 and 36. If you do ride, in Nevada, you are not allowed to drive between cars and it cools down significantly at night so don't forget your leather jacket even if it's 80 degrees during the day.

You can also get to Reno using **Greyhound** or **Amtrak**. While trains seem nostalgic and romantic, I hear it's very slow. Greyhound has really large, nice coaches now. Remember the old days of aluminum-sided buses no larger than city buses? We also now have **Megabus** from downtown Sparks to Sacramento and San Francisco. If you're the first to get tickets, they're only $1! Why are they so cheap? They don't have bus station overhead. As of January 2018, however, they are suspending Reno service.

What is Crime Like in Reno?

You're more likely to get mugged by a one-armed bandit than a real thug. (A one-armed bandit is a slot machine, get it?) For a city of our size, we have relatively low crime in all categories. In 2014, Reno had 1,147 violent crimes, 15 murders/non-negligent manslaughter, 128 reported rapes, and 263 robberies. Stockton, CA by comparison with 70K more residents had 3,988 violent crimes, 49 murders/non-negligent manslaughter, 134 reported rapes, and 1,098 robberies. A woman can walk up and down Virginia Street downtown at midnight and be just fine. We had a nasty gang problem back in 1995, but it's rare to hear about a gang shooting or drive-by these days. There are a few panhandlers here and there, but they're nowhere as aggressive as San Francisco's. Also, keep in mind, most panhandlers are NOT homeless, and most homeless do NOT panhandle. And most panhandlers are alcoholics or drug addicts and will NOT spend your money on food. If you want to be Mother Theresa, go feed the homeless at a soup kitchen or donate an old coat or $20 to some homeless shelter. Giving a dollar to a panhandler is a selfish act. You are enabling him, and the only reason you did it was either because you were scared or guilty, but you didn't care that he'd turn the corner, buy some liquor and pass out in the cold, possibly to die. If you really want to feed him, ask him to follow you to a convenience store and buy him a sandwich.

This still has a small town feel, but of course, don't be stupid. Don't get all wasted and stumble around downtown at 3 AM by yourself. I wouldn't park on the street downtown on a Friday or Saturday night. A lot of casinos have free parking or better yet valet and tip the valet dudes.

Some people think Reno has ghettos, but I'm positive these people are from small towns like Yerington and Patrick. I've been to Oakland, South Central, West Philadelphia, South Chicago, the Florida panhandle, the Bronx, Khayelitsha, and Reno does not have ghettos. We have poor city neighborhoods spanning no more than several blocks. We have the North Valleys which are vast tracts of low income rural folk, but they mind their own business, and they are not ghettos.

Where Should I Live in Reno?

Much like every other city in America, the further out you go, the nicer the neighborhoods with the exception of the North Valleys which have traditionally been the home of poorer and more rural whites. While they don't all wear cowboy hats up there, many live in trailers and drive pick-ups with pit-bulls. As a proponent of smart growth and sustainability, I recommend living as close to where you work as possible or downtown or Midtown, at least within the McCarran Loop. But if you have kids, I can't argue with your logic if you want your kids to go to a newer, nicer school. Sparks is what I consider a boring bedroom community, but there are nice neighborhoods in the Northeast and then Spanish Springs (north of Sparks).

While older people like to move to downtown in part, because they don't have kids and have to worry about school districts, keep in mind, the drunks and homeless were there before you were. You can't outlaw homelessness and in a casino town, you can't outlaw bars being open past 2 AM. Unfortunately, there are recent laws outlawing homeless people from sitting or sleeping downtown or camping down by the river. If you don't like seeing homeless people sleeping downtown, that is your problem not theirs. That is the face of reality and modern society, and most homeless people mind their own business. Homeless are often the most vulnerable and weak, and they sleep on sidewalks to protect themselves from predators who would otherwise prey upon them in dark alleys, parks, or hidden away. A mentally challenged homeless woman was raped and killed in a restroom in a park in Reno a few years ago. Is that where you want them to sleep? Out-of-sight-out-of-mind is a selfish, evil way to live.

If you're somewhere in the middle, the old Southwest inside the McCarran Loop is okay except for the area around the Peppermill. The area just southeast of downtown is fine. Northwest Reno outside the McCarran Loop is nice. There is a nice development called Sonterra at Sommerset, however, further west of Northwest. The old Northwest inside the McCarran Loop is fine as is old Sparks inside the McCarran Loop. Here are some neighborhoods to avoid, basically areas around these streets: Neil Rd, Grove St, Wedekind Rd, Montello St, and Brinkby Ave.

How Expensive is Reno?

Up until this edition, I would have said Reno is relatively cheap, but the local real estate boom has changed all that. Both our blessing and curse is that we live next door to the virtual nation of California. During the Great Recession, a 3-bedroom 2,000 sq. ft. house was going for $200K. Good luck finding any house under $300K now. A nice, clean one-bedroom here goes for about $1,200/month. Keep in mind, with all these investment properties you can rent a house or condo too.

You will save money on gas, because everything is so close, and there's barely any traffic. You will save money at restaurants and bars. A $20 meal in Reno is $40 in San Francisco, somewhere in the middle in Sacramento. There are plenty of cheap beer specials especially in the casinos. You may lose about $150 booking any airplane trip, because we always have to go through San Francisco, Vegas, Phoenix, or Dallas. But then again, taking a Lyft to the airport is cheaper, and you don't waste an hour in line.

Because Renoites don't flash their wealth around, there's very little pressure to outdo your neighbors, peers, coworkers, or friends. In fact, often you'll find yourself dressing down and talking modestly about your material wealth. Nobody fricking wears suits here unless you work in a casino, you're attending a funeral or wedding, or you're attending a rare formal party, and even then, 90% of Renoites wear sport jackets and mismatched pants even to a black tie party instead of tuxedos. You shouldn't be surprised to see a cowboy hat and bolo there too.

What's the Local Political Scene Like?

Until the 2012 election, the old school network of gaming was running the show in Reno despite the fact that casino hotel employment makes up 7% of the total work force as opposed to 16% in 1996. There was a time when it made up a huge portion of our economy, but Reno's economy has since diversified and with Vegas dominating, Indian Casinos, Internet gambling, and legalized gaming in other states, Reno's gaming and tourism sector will continue to shrink both absolutely and proportionately.

Unfortunately, our old beloved, city leaders along with the vast majority of city voters lived in the past and still listen to Lawrence Welk. As a result of this, they have heavily gambled on downtown redevelopment where most of our casinos sit. The Reno-Sparks Convention and Visitors Authority (RSCVA) was created in 1959 and unlike other convention and visitor bureaus across the country, owns and operates tourism facilities, specifically, the Reno-Sparks Convention Center (across from the Atlantis), the Reno Events Center (downtown), the National Bowling Stadium (downtown), the Reno-Sparks Livestock Events Center (northeast Reno), and the Reno Ballroom (downtown). If you are observant, you noticed that none of these facilities are in Sparks, yet the RSCVA collects room taxes from hotels in Sparks as well. Can you say shafted? There is also now a $2 room tax on downtown hotels to pay to remodel the National Bowling Stadium. In addition to this, in 2005, Reno lowered the railroad tracks that cut right through downtown, digging a trench that now costs us $634 million (according to Reno News & Review). Taxpayers are and will finance this trench through hotel room taxes, a special downtown assessment district, a sales tax increase, a city bond, and federal grants.

Then there have been additional projects (Cabela's sporting goods store for Reno and Scheels sporting goods store for Sparks, interestingly both competing with each other) funded through something called STAR (Sales Tax Anticipation Revenue) bonds allowing government to borrow against the projected sales-tax revenues inside a special tourism district and then 75% of the sales taxes it generates would pay off the STAR bond debt. I call it Stolen Taxes Allocated to the Rich. The City has also financed the new Aces Baseball Stadium and Freight House Complex with taxes and bonds. Another problem I have with these huge redevelopment projects is that they reallocate wealth from all of us to a few lucky, influential developers and corporations. Did Reno or Sparks care that the mega-sporting goods stores would put small, independently owned sporting goods stores out of business? Across the country, these unelected redevelopment agencies with eminent domain powers are swindling us, throwing people out of their homes and businesses, and redistributing wealth. Have you ever once considered visiting Boise, Butte, Cheyenne, Bend, Flagstaff, or Ogden because they have some fancy big redevelopment project or some mega-chain store? Then why would people regionally visit Reno because we have Scheels or the Freight House district? California Governor Jerry Brown smartly eliminated all redevelopment agencies in California. Wake up Nevada!

Not only is it foolhardy for taxpayers of Reno to invest in a dying industry, but it is also unfair to all the other sectors in Reno that do not get subsidies or government projects benefiting them. Where are the huge subsidies and projects for construction, manufacturing, retail, restaurants, bars, transportation, warehousing, insurance, professional services, healthcare, or high tech? I don't actually support any government subsidies for particular sectors, however, if you want bang for your buck, investing in technology is probably a hundred times better than gaming and tourism. Reno has great potential for being a low-tax, hi-tech hub being so close to Silicon Valley. We are doing nothing to make this happen but increasing taxes and debt for everyone. Ultimately, we will have to raise taxes to cover our debts, and that is when no company will move to Reno for low taxes and Reno will self-implode.

If you want a perfect example of free market at work that is not subsidized by government and redevelopment agencies just look at what is happening with Midtown Reno. No convention center, no government financed entertainment complex, no government incentivized package for some huge chain department store, no trench, no sports stadium, just small, independent businesses creating a beautiful, cohesive, eclectic, exciting, fun, thriving neighborhood. That's free market folks.

The pre-2012 City Council struck a deal with Apple to locate an office complex downtown and a server farm east of Sparks for major tax breaks. While Renoites may celebrate this, it smacks of corporate welfare, and if every city in America gave big companies tax breaks to locate in their cities, big companies would never have to pay their fair share of taxes. You can't be too big to tax. In 2014, the State of Nevada passed legislation in defiance of the state constitution to give Tesla $1.25 billion in tax breaks to open a battery plant in the Tahoe-Reno Industrial Center (TRI), and in what may possibly be the funniest coincidences, the guy who created TRI also owns the Mustang Ranch in the same county.

In 2014, Reno voted for Hillary Schieve, a Midtown business owner, over the chairman of the Builders Association of Nevada, a resounding defeat for the old boy's network and urban sprawl. It was similar to the election of managed-growth candidate Barbara Bennett in 1979, Reno's first female mayor. Unfortunately, Schieve has continued to focus on downtown special interests to the neglect of the rest of the city, spearheading cruel laws to ban sitting or sleeping on downtown sidewalks. Instead of simply accepting the fact that downtown gaming and tourism is in decline and has been for decades, we shift all the blame on homeless people "scaring off tourists." This is beyond vile.

FAQs

Can I smoke pot in Reno?

As of January 1, 2017, possession of up to one ounce of marijuana is legal. However, some jurisdictions in Nevada will continue to prosecute you for possession of any quantity of marijuana. The City of Reno District Attorney stated that he will no longer prosecute for possession under one ounce, while the City of Sparks and Washoe County District Attorneys stated that they will. Always safer than sorry.

Can I get a hooker in Reno?

Yes, you can walk down to the casino bar or the street and find a street hooker, and it is perfectly illegal, and besides getting some hideous venereal disease, you might get a citation or go to jail. Embarrassing! Nevada has legal brothels but only in certain counties, and Washoe County is not one of them. Nearby Carson and Storey Counties both allow and have legal brothels. I hear the workers there get tested each month and yes, I have been to one and no, I have not partaken in the forbidden yet entirely legal fruit. There's a whole menu of what you can get for how long and for how much.

There is the very famous **Mustang Ranch** and **Wild Horse** in Patrick (the city, not Sponge Bob's pal) that are only 17 miles from downtown Reno. Wild Horse has a strip club where you can see the goods before taking them for a ride. There's also the **Kit Kat Ranch, Moonlite Bunny Ranch, Love Ranch,** and **Sagebrush Ranch** in Mound House which is about five miles northeast of Carson City which is 30 miles south of Reno. Any taxi in Reno will be more than obliging to drive you all the way there as they get some sort of kickback for their efforts as well as Uber and Lyft. You can actually go on some of the brothel websites to check out their workers and call ahead for availability. As I understand it, they will quote you a price, but tips, as in most all service industries, are greatly appreciated.

Can I drink an open container downtown?

No. Our fearful municipal leaders decided to put an end to this wonderful tradition. If you seem reasonable and respectful, they will kindly ask you to dump out your booze as you profusely apologize and tell them how much you gamble and love the town. Also, keep in mind, jaywalking is frowned upon and you could get a ticket, and god forbid you act like a fool, you will spend the night not in your hotel room, but a smelly, cold jail for public intoxication, disturbing the peace, or interfering with the duties of a police officer.

What's the sales tax?

Washoe County sales tax is 8.265%. Can you say boiling frog?

When can I drink and where can I buy alcohol?

You can drink 24-hours-a-day, any day of the week at any place that says they are open, restaurants included. You can buy liquor in any liquor store, gas station, convenience store, wine store, restaurant, or grocery store any day of the week, any hour of the day so long as they are open. God bless Nevada!

What do locals think of tourists?

When you tell someone you've lived in Reno seven years, you're virtually a native. Most folks have just moved here, and from California, so they don't really think any differently about you as they did a few years back when they were your neighbors. If you're a rich dude wearing a suit, locals will think you work in the casinos. You guys allow us not to pay state income taxes, so for the most part, we are happy you are here losing all your money.

Are Renoites racist?

There are Renoites born here or who grew up in rural Northern Nevada, and unless they're hip hop fans, they're a bit weirded out by large groups of minorities, especially those who dress like gangsters. But for the most part, they really don't care especially the younger they get. Since Reno is also half comprised of Californians which is a multi-racial state, they're used to different races. In fact, in California today, whites are the minorities. Also, since Reno is comprised of mostly new settlers, we're a lot more open and inclusive to all. There are no hate groups in Reno that I know of. There are no militias for that matter. As open and cool Seattleites and Portlandungerheads are, they have hate groups up there. I have traveled the world, and I would honestly say Reno is one of the least racist and most inclusive places. But let's not get carried away, most people who grew up here never had Asian or black friends, and some are passively racist. "Why don't they be speaking American instead of Mexican?"

Is Reno homophobic?

Being so close to Gay'ol San Franny, people here are used to gays and have no problem with them. I've never heard of a single gay-bashing incident here the 21 years I've been here. We are also not very religious and our existing religions tend not to be fundamentalist. If anything,

Reno has a homeless bashing problem. Two homeless people were murdered by non-homeless people in 2007 and 2009.

What's the smoking policy in Reno?

Most Cali's will be shocked to find out that we can actually smoke nearly everywhere, except in restaurants. The people voted to ban smoking in bars where they serve food, but Governor Sandoval overturned it. You can smoke in parks, on the sidewalk, in parking lots, up people's butts.

What's the gun policy in Reno?

Reno is a pretty gun friendly place. We have a Concealed Carry Weapon law that requires a background check, basic safety course, and basic target shooting. We honor many other state permits. Check online to make sure. You can carry open, but I wouldn't recommend it, and some casinos ban pistols both open and concealed. You can carry concealed anywhere except court buildings and wherever the business or organization posts a sign banning them. However, I have a natural habit of ignoring any sign posted near any entrance. Better to be judged by twelve than carried by six is what I say Marty. You cannot carry concealed and get drunk of course, although you can carry inside a bar. You can transport a fully loaded pistol or rifle in your vehicle within arm's reach or even open on a seat. You cannot shoot someone sleeping in your bed or car.

What's the speed limit on Reno freeways?

65 MPH but since our freeways are virtually in a constant state of reconstruction and expansion, be on the lookout for 55 MPH work zones.

When, where, and how much do you tip?

Tourists often forget that you should tip your valet not only after picking your car up but before to make sure he treats your car well. $1 before and after is fine, but I like to tip $2. Also, you should always tip the cocktail waitress who gives you free drinks at the casinos no matter how long it takes her to get you a drink. It's not her fault but the casino's. Personally, in a really busy bar I tip prompt waitresses and bartenders $2 to stand out from the crowd and ensure better service, and keep in mind, because of inflation, a $1 tip today is really like tipping someone 50 cents in 1987. Of course, bartenders complain that people who were drinking in 1987 tip them 50 cents today. I hope I'm not the old codger in 2030 who still tips $1. When you're playing table games, don't forget to tip the dealer if you're winning. You can also put money on the table on the dealer's behalf and some enjoy being part of the action. If there's a long line going into a bar or club, sometimes you can tip security $5 or $10 per person to skip the line depending on how long the line is, but be discreet because management may not approve of the practice.

Random Historical and Weird Stuff about Reno

- Back in the day, the front entrances of many casinos were in alleys like Douglas and Fulton Alleys. I'm sure they didn't store their garbage bins in the alleys, and it smelled a hundred times better and was much better lit. You'll see this same concept in many European cities where they will even have tables set out in the alleys. With Americans so used to garbage bins and crackheads sleeping and shitting in alleys, it might take a while for us to get used to the idea of eating a nice dinner in an alley.

- On July 4th, 1910, legendary black boxer **Jack Johnson** fought James Jeffries, the former boxing great and the "great white hope" to beat Johnson and regain white manly glory. Johnson dominated the fight, and Jeffries' corner threw in the great white towel.

- There were a lot of local breweries back in the mining days. Reno's first brewery was **"Reno Brewery"** on Commercial Row and opened in 1868 by German immigrant Frederick Hertlein. German immigrants monopolized the beer industry in Reno as well as elsewhere, much like the Chinese had their restaurants and the Irish had their bars and police precincts. There were also beer depots where out-of-state brewers sent beer to Reno on trains to get bottled, kegged, and sold here or reshipped by wagon or truck to towns inaccessible by train. After 1900, one of the leading depots was Rainier Bottling Works of the Seattle Brewing and Malting Co (also maker of the famed Rainier beer) located on Spokane Street. The name of the street is probably based on the fact that Rainier in Seattle is located just north of their Spokane Street. One of the bottling buildings remains there today, and the Spice House strip club used to be a brewery or part of the bottling company. Of course, Prohibition destroyed a lot of breweries and beer depots, and then larger national breweries put the rest out of business. The **Reno Brewing Company**'s renowned Sierra Beer disappeared in 1957. Then in the 90's microbrews made a comeback.

- November 24, 1971, a man who became known as **D. B. Cooper** pulled off perhaps the only successful airplane hijacking if in fact he jumped and lived. He hijacked a plane from Seattle that landed in Reno.

- The Sparks Nugget used to have an Asian elephant named **Bertha**.

- **Johnny Cash** never really shot a man in Reno to watch him die.

- **Lionel Richie** and **Diana Ross** recorded "Endless Love" in a Reno recording studio. It initially was not a duet, and Ross ended up singing the guy's part.

- For ages, we misspelled "Sadleir" Way "Sadlier" Told you, random

- UNR's Agriculture School has a history of alleged animal abuse. When a professor blew the whistle, they fired him. It didn't help that his name was Hussein S. Hussein. There was also flooding once, and they were very casual about letting a lot of animals drown.

- Unknown to most Americans, 24 US universities house and operate nuclear reactors. Unknown to most Renoites, a 14-year-old named **Taylor Wilson** built a nuclear reactor in Reno and became the youngest person in history to produce nuclear fusion. At 15, the US Department of Homeland Security invited him to their offices perhaps to amuse themselves and give him a sticker, but he startled them when he used his cheap homemade Geiger counter to show them their building was radioactive.

- If you still think Renoites are stupid, we're home to **Digital Solid State Propulsion, LLC.** which manufactures guided missile and space vehicle propulsion units and parts. Sparks is home to Sierra Nevada Corp. which created the **Dream Chaser**, according to Wikipedia, a "reusable crewed suborbital and orbital vertical-takeoff, horizontal-landing lifting-body spaceplane." **Ormat Technologies** based in Reno is a global leader in geothermal fracking technology.

- Cadillac Lounge used to be **Peyton Place** which was a swinging swinger's club. Cadillac Lounge is named after Cadillac cars but Lincoln Lounge down the street is named after a dead president.

- The first American Tour de France winner, **Greg LeMond**, grew up in Reno. Reno's high altitude and Lake Tahoe's great mountain climbs certainly helped prepare him to become the greatest cyclist of the world.

- Kietzke is pronounced "kit-ski". Oh and hey everyone, it's 40 fricking MPH on Kietzke STOP DOING 30!!!!!!!!!!!!

- Kuenzli is pronounced "koons-lee" not "kuntslee"

- Nevada is pronounced "Ne-VAHH-dah" rhyming with ladder, not "Nir-VADA" rhyming with empanada, or "Neh-VEIGH-da" like you're Kiwi or something. For the correct pronunciation, refer to this Youtube video:

  http://www.youtube.com/watch?v=vpW_F56AM1k

I paid the dude $5 to make that video.

- Since naming a street "Martin Luther King, Jnr." reduces property value on that street by 99%, Reno decided to name a section of US 395/I-580, Martin Luther King, Jr. Memorial Highway.

- When in Reno, anyone says stuff like, "How are the bars in Stead?" I go, "Instead of what?" It never gets old, NEVER. Solid gold.

- They say that **Sun Valley** is the largest trailer park capital in America, but I somehow doubt that having visited the Florida panhandle. They say that Sun Valley has the most ex-con's per capita, well, that may be true, but in reality, Sun Valley is not all that bad. I have seen poverty in Stockton, California and the South, and I just don't think Sun Valley is bad. Heck, I've seen poverty in Mexico and South Africa. Fact is, if you own your own trailer home in Sun Valley and a pickup, you're richer than 90% of the people in the world. And I'd rather walk down Sun Valley Bl at night any night than South Central, LA or the Bronx or Oakland although have you noticed the hipster bars in downtown Oakland?

- Reno and Nevada lead America in suicides, tobacco use, alcoholism, high school dropouts, teenage pregnancy, gambling addiction (of course), and bankruptcies, and we're damn proud of it. We're fricking survivors man, well, besides the suicide thing. Actually, my theory behind this is that when Reno and Nevada were the fastest growing places in America, we attracted a lot of transient people, explorers, and drifters and many people moving here left the safety and security of their families and social networks behind.

- High altitude deprives the brain of oxygen and for a lot of people it enhances the effects of alcohol. On top of that, when tourists come to Reno, the lack of oxygen taxes their bodies more, making them more vulnerable to the effects of alcohol and drugs. Be careful.

- The former owner of the Sparks Nugget, **John Ascuaga** is Basque. His restaurant Orozko was named after the city in Spain from where his father came.

- **Zombo** is a crazy zombie dude with a weird Eastern European accent who hosts old horror movie shows.

- There used to be a dude who walked around Reno waving at everybody and then later the one-eyed skateboard dude.

- In 2012, the Reno Police Department murdered Alfred, this police groupie who used to constantly pester the cops. He had become increasingly aggressive and started stealing things out of police cars, so one day they trapped him inside a police car and had him euthanized. I probably should mention that Alfred was a crow.

- We have **Job Corps** up in Stead (of where?) which provides free education and vocational training and residential housing to youth age 16 to 24. Job Corps was President Johnson's central program in his "War on Poverty." We seem to be losing that war. Although, a lot of Job Corps kids come from California and get a bad reputation from locals, I've met a few and you have to give them credit for at least trying to get an education and improve their lives. One of my closest friends was in Job Corps. When I was in Sacramento, I even considered going to Job Corps (as well as Peace Corps) but they said the winters in Reno sucked, and then I eventually moved to Reno.

- Here's a bunch of movies that have parts of Reno or have been shot in parts of Reno: *Misfits, Sister Act, Love Ranch, El Cortez, The Cooler, Kingpin, Balls of Fury, the Muppets,* and *Waking Up in Reno.* Reno really isn't featured prominently in *Balls of Fury* or *Kingpin,* both pretty funny movies, but by far the best Reno movie is **Hard Eight** starring **Gwyneth Paltrow**. It has nice shots of the old Flamingo Hilton. *The Cooler* is depressing and *El Cortez,* besides Lou Diamond Philip's great acting, sucks balls of fury. This is how cool Renoites are. When they were filming a scene where some dude was beating up someone, a guy walking by thought it was real and tried to save the "victim." When they were filming *El Cortez,* I kid you not, I walked right through a street scene having no clue I was walking through their set. That's how rarely Hollywood comes to Reno. BTW, the scene was cut.

- People from Reno like to be called "Renoites" not butt hats.

- Borrowing from Northern Cal, we say "**hella**" here a hella lot, as in "There are hella tat shops here," or "That was a hella good band."

- **DILLIGAS** bar stands for Do I Look Like I Give A Shit

- Reno had a very active, vocal watchdog, **Sam Dehne**. He used to rail against the excesses and corruption of the Council and Mayor for decades, however, his pompous self-promotion and tendency to play his guitar and sing at City Council meetings undermined his credibility. Never trust anyone who speaks about himself in the third-person.

Ten Reno Scandals and Calamities

1. On Thanksgiving Day, 1980, nutjob, Priscilla Ford drove her car onto the sidewalks downtown and killed six people and injured 23. This is why you'll see all the concrete and metal garbage can holders and adornments downtown on Virginia Street. Coincidentally, the Lincoln Continental she was driving was made by Ford. Coincidentally too, a woman named Priscilla Alden supposedly celebrated the first Thanksgiving in the Plymouth Colony. Not coincidentally the Plymouth car is made by Chrysler.

2. January 21, 1985, a 4-engine turboprop airliner, Galaxy Airlines Flight 203 crashed about 1.5 miles from the airport after taking off killing 70 on board. Only one person, George Lamson, Jr. survived. Nobody on the ground was killed. Some people would say the sole survivor was a miracle, but seriously, unless the airplane is nose-diving from 30K feet into the side of a mountain, many, many people do survive plane crashes, and odds are the number starts from one and goes up to everybody on board. Every year, the freaked out Renoites used to conduct a mass-casualty reenactment called "Broken Arrow" which soon became more like a Civil War reenactment so they stopped doing it. The sole survivor stayed in Reno and became a casino dealer. CNN made a film called *Sole Survivor* starring Lamson, Jr. as he reached out to other sole survivors of airplane crashes.

3. August 12, 1995, 12-year-old Jessica Arenas was shot and killed by a gang member's stray bullet at a local park sparking community-wide outrage and activism against crime and gang violence during the worst year of gang violence Reno had ever experienced. This also brought about Reno's first Guardian Angels chapter.

4. We had a small riot here during Hot August Nights in 1998. I was there, no not rioting. It wasn't anything like the LA Riots which I also experienced. A car was flipped over, barricades were thrown down, garbage cans thrown around and a few windows were broken. You see, before that, Hot August Nights became a huge youth party for tourists, and from the Bay, especially, and there were more blacks and Latinos than Renoites were comfortable with, so they took the riots which were perpetrated by people of all colors as an excuse to crack down on that big youth party. The funny thing about Hot August Nights is that each year, the classic car definition ages another year, so pretty soon, instead of a bunch of old white folk in T-birds and '55 Chevy's, we will soon see a bunch of rich old

Latinos and blacks in restored 60's and 70's Cadillac's and then 80's Buicks. One day, there will be 70-year-old Asians in restored, tuned up 00's Honda Civics reliving their glory days of drifting.

5. January 30, 2000, the City blew up the Mapes Hotel, built in 1947. It was the last major American building created in the art deco style.

6. Palace Pawn Shop in downtown Reno has the unfortunate legacy of its owner Darren Mack going crazy on June 12, 2006, and killing his wife in an ugly divorce case and then taking a rifle and shooting and wounding his divorce judge from across the street in a parking garage.

7. July 8, 2006, Nevada State Controller and State Treasurer candidate Kathy Augustine was found unconscious in her home in Reno and died four days later. Following an investigation, her husband was convicted of murdering her using succinylcholine, a paralyzing drug.

8. Halloween 2006, Valerie Moore set fire to a mattress in a hallway at the Mizpah Hotel which ended up burning up the entire place and killing twelve people. She was angry at her ex-boyfriend, and I'm thinking, just frickin unfriend him on Facebook!

9. January 20, 2008, 19-year-old Brianna Denison was abducted from a friend's house near the University of Nevada and killed by James Biela. Biela was not arrested until November of that year causing widespread fear especially amongst college students. Biela was also convicted of sexual assault and attempted rape of another woman. That woman had a concealed weapons permit, but because the University brain trust banned concealed weapons on campus, she was unable to carry one when she was attacked.

10. September 16, 2011 at the Reno Air Races in Stead, one of the competition racing planes, a P51D Mustang, crashed into a spectator area and killed ten people on the ground and the pilot. Another pilot was killed in the race in 1999; however, no spectators were killed or injured.

Final Words of Advice

There's this old story of a dude who visits New York City for the first time, and he asks his Uber driver how he thinks he'll get along with New York, because he's heard all these wonderful things about the town like the food and culture, and everyone is helpful and outgoing. The Uber driver tells him that he will love New York, meet many friends, and sorely miss it when he leaves. Another dude arrives in New York City for the first time, and he asks the Uber driver if he thinks he'll enjoy the place, because he's heard it is full of crime, traffic, loud and rude people, racial conflict, everyone is in a rush to get somewhere, and they all hate tourists. The Uber driver drives him to the Bronx and mugs and kills him. No, seriously, the Uber driver tells him that he will not enjoy his time here, he should stick closely to his hotel, and he will be happy to leave.

The moral of the story is that you get out what you put in. It's just like Burning Man. If you think Burning Man will be a horrible experience, it probably will be. If you think an acid trip will make you go raving nuts and smash your head into walls and jump out of second floor windows, you probably will have a very bad trip. Reno is what you want to make out of it. You can look around for junkies, closed stores, brownfields, signs of dilapidation and despair, and I guarantee you will find them all. You can also look around for unexpected gems, great restaurants, fun bars, and wonderful people, and I guarantee you will find them all too.

It is only too human of us to project ourselves not only on to other cities and our environment but other people. If someone is not talking to you much, you can view him as a hostile, stuck up, condescending ass who thinks he is better than you, or you can view him as a shy, uncertain, yet friendly and interesting person if you can only break the ice. We like to think of ourselves as victims of our circumstances, our cities, and this allows us the comfort of sitting back and doing nothing but complain. We can also think of ourselves as agents of our own fate, of cities as our playgrounds, of people as magic boxes full of amazing features and potentially fun shared experiences. Reno can be your playground, and its people can be magical. Or it can also be a chafed taint. As with culture shock, it can be an endless struggle with language, misunderstandings, taboos, mistakes, disturbances, inconveniences, and frustration, or it can be a wonderful adventure full of fresh perspectives, funny anecdotes, small triumphs, earned respect, and humility. But it really is all up to you.

Made in the USA
San Bernardino, CA
12 August 2019